T0260591

Data Pipelines Pocket Reference

Moving and Processing Data for Analytics

James Densmore

Beijing · Boston · Farnham · Sebastopol · Tokyo

Data Pipelines Pocket Reference

by James Densmore

Printed in the United States of America.

Published by O'Reilly Media, Inc., 1005 Gravenstein Highway North, Sebastopol, CA 95472.

O'Reilly books may be purchased for educational, business, or sales promotional use. Online editions are also available for most titles (*http://oreilly.com*). For more information, contact our corporate/institutional sales department: 800-998-9938 or *corporate@oreilly.com*.

Acquisitions Editor: Jessica Haberman
Developmental Editor: Corbin Collins
Production Editor: Katherine Tozer
Copyeditor: Kim Wimpsett
Proofreader: Abby Wheeler
Indexer: Ellen Troutman
Interior Designer: David Futato
Cover Designer: Karen Montgomery
Illustrator: Kate Dullea

March 2021:   First Edition

Revision History for the First Edition
    2021-02-10:   First Release

See   *http://oreilly.com/catalog/errata.csp?isbn=9781492087830*   for   release details.

978-1-492-08783-0

[LSI]

Table of Contents

Preface

Data pipelines are the foundation for success in data analytics and machine learning. Moving data from numerous, diverse sources and processing it to provide context is the difference between having data and getting value from it.

I've worked as a data analyst, data engineer, and leader in the data analytics field for more than 10 years. In that time, I've seen rapid change and growth in the field. The emergence of cloud infrastructure, and cloud data warehouses in particular, has created an opportunity to rethink the way data pipelines are designed and implemented.

This book describes what I believe are the foundations and best practices of building data pipelines in the modern era. I base my opinions and observations on my own experience as well as those of industry leaders who I know and follow.

My goal is for this book to serve as a blueprint as well as a reference. While your needs are specific to your organization and the problems you've set out to solve, I've found success with variations of these foundations many times over. I hope you find it a valuable resource in your journey to building and maintaining data pipelines that power your data organization.

Who This Book Is For

This book's primary audience is current and aspiring data engineers as well as analytics team members who want to understand what data pipelines are and how they are implemented. Their job titles include data engineers, technical leads, data warehouse engineers, analytics engineers, business intelligence engineers, and director/VP-level analytics leaders.

I assume that you have a basic understanding of data warehousing concepts. To implement the examples discussed, you should be comfortable with SQL databases, REST APIs, and JSON. You should be proficient in a scripting language, such as Python. Basic knowledge of the Linux command line and at least one cloud computing platform is ideal as well.

All code samples are written in Python and SQL and make use of many open source libraries. I use Amazon Web Services (AWS) to demonstrate the techniques described in the book, and AWS services are used in many of the code samples. When possible, I note similar services on other major cloud providers such as Microsoft Azure and Google Cloud Platform (GCP). All code samples can be modified for the cloud provider of your choice, as well as for on-premises use.

Conventions Used in This Book

The following typographical conventions are used in this book:

Italic

> Indicates new terms, URLs, email addresses, filenames, and file extensions.

`Constant width`

> Used for program listings, as well as within paragraphs to refer to program elements such as variable or function names, databases, data types, environment variables, statements, and keywords.

Constant width bold

> Shows commands or other text that should be typed literally by the user.

Constant width italic

> Shows text that should be replaced with user-supplied values or by values determined by context.

Using Code Examples

Supplemental material (code examples, exercises, etc.) is available for download at *https://oreil.ly/datapipelinescode*.

If you have a technical question or a problem using the code examples, please send email to *bookquestions@oreilly.com*.

This book is here to help you get your job done. In general, if example code is offered with this book, you may use it in your programs and documentation. You do not need to contact us for permission unless you're reproducing a significant portion of the code. For example, writing a program that uses several chunks of code from this book does not require permission. Selling or distributing examples from O'Reilly books does require permission. Answering a question by citing this book and quoting example code does not require permission. Incorporating a significant amount of example code from this book into your product's documentation does require permission.

We appreciate, but generally do not require, attribution. An attribution usually includes the title, author, publisher, and ISBN. For example: "*Data Pipelines Pocket Reference* by James Densmore (O'Reilly). Copyright 2021 James Densmore, 978-1-492-08783-0."

If you feel your use of code examples falls outside fair use or the permission given above, please feel free to contact us: *permissions@oreilly.com*.

O'Reilly Online Learning

O'REILLY® For more than 40 years, *O'Reilly Media* has provided technology and business training, knowledge, and insight to help companies succeed.

Our unique network of experts and innovators share their knowledge and expertise through books, articles, and our online learning platform. O'Reilly's online learning platform gives you on-demand access to live training courses, in-depth learning paths, interactive coding environments, and a vast collection of text and video from O'Reilly and 200+ other publishers. For more information, visit *http://oreilly.com*.

How to Contact Us

Please address comments and questions concerning this book to the publisher:

O'Reilly Media, Inc.
1005 Gravenstein Highway North
Sebastopol, CA 95472
800-998-9938 (in the United States or Canada)
707-829-0515 (international or local)
707-829-0104 (fax)

We have a web page for this book, where we list errata, examples, and any additional information. You can access this page at *https://oreil.ly/data-pipelines-pocket-ref*.

Email *bookquestions@oreilly.com* to comment or ask technical questions about this book.

For news and information about our books and courses, visit *http://oreilly.com*.

Find us on Facebook: *http://facebook.com/oreilly*

Follow us on Twitter: *http://twitter.com/oreillymedia*

Watch us on YouTube: *http://www.youtube.com/oreillymedia*

Acknowledgments

Thank you to everyone at O'Reilly who helped make this book possible, especially Jessica Haberman and Corbin Collins. The invaluable feedback of three amazing technical reviewers, Joy Payton, Gordon Wong, and Scott Haines led to critical improvements throughout. Finally, thank you to my wife Amanda for her encouragement from the moment this book was proposed, as well as my dog Izzy for sitting by my side during countless hours of writing.

## CHAPTER 1

Introduction to Data Pipelines

Behind every glossy dashboard, machine learning model, and business-changing insight is data. Not just raw data, but data collected from numerous sources that must be cleaned, processed, and combined to deliver value. The famous phrase "data is the new oil" has proven true. Just like oil, the value of data is in its potential after it's refined and delivered to the consumer. Also like oil, it takes efficient pipelines to deliver data through each stage of its value chain.

This Pocket Reference discusses what these data pipelines are and shows how they fit into a modern data ecosystem. It covers common considerations and key decision points when implementing pipelines, such as batch versus streaming data ingestion, building versus buying tooling, and more. Though it is not exclusive to a single language or platform, it addresses the most common decisions made by data professionals while discussing foundational concepts that apply to homegrown solutions, open source frameworks, and commercial products.

What Are Data Pipelines?

Data pipelines are sets of processes that move and transform data from various sources to a destination where new value can be derived. They are the foundation of analytics, reporting, and machine learning capabilities.

The complexity of a data pipeline depends on the size, state, and structure of the source data as well as the needs of the analytics project. In their simplest form, pipelines may extract only data from one source such as a REST API and load to a destination such as a SQL table in a data warehouse. In practice, however, pipelines typically consist of multiple steps including data extraction, data preprocessing, data validation, and at times training or running a machine learning model before delivering data to its final destination. Pipelines often contain tasks from multiple systems and programming languages. What's more, data teams typically own and maintain numerous data pipelines that share dependencies and must be coordinated. Figure 1-1 illustrates a simple pipeline.

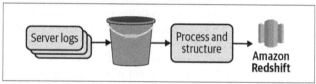

Figure 1-1. A simple pipeline that loads server log data into an S3 Bucket, does some basic processing and structuring, and loads the results into an Amazon Redshift database.

Who Builds Data Pipelines?

With the popularization of cloud computing and software as a service (SaaS), the number of data sources organizations need to make sense of has exploded. At the same time, the demand for data to feed machine learning models, data science research, and time-sensitive insights is higher than ever. To keep up, *data engineering* has emerged as a key role on analytics teams. *Data engineers* specialize in building and maintaining the data pipelines that underpin the analytics ecosystem.

A data engineer's purpose isn't simply to load data into a data warehouse. Data engineers work closely with data scientists and analysts to understand what will be done with the data and help bring their needs into a scalable production state.

Data engineers take pride in ensuring the validity and timeliness of the data they deliver. That means testing, alerting, and creating contingency plans for when something goes wrong. And yes, something will eventually go wrong!

The specific skills of a data engineer depend somewhat on the tech stack their organization uses. However, there are some common skills that all good data engineers possess.

SQL and Data Warehousing Fundamentals

Data engineers need to know how to query databases, and SQL is the universal language to do so. Experienced data engineers know how to write high-performance SQL and understand the fundamentals of data warehousing and data modeling. Even if a data team includes data warehousing specialists, a data engineer with warehousing fundamentals is a better partner and can fill more complex technical gaps that arise.

Python and/or Java

The language in which a data engineer is proficient will depend on the tech stack of their team, but either way a data engineer isn't going to get the job done with "no code" tools even if they have some good ones in their arsenal. Python and Java currently dominate in data engineering, but newcomers like Go are emerging.

Distributed Computing

Solving a problem that involves high data volume and a desire to process data quickly has led data engineers to work with *distributed computing* platforms. Distributed computing combines the power of multiple systems to efficiently store, process, and analyze high volumes of data.

One popular example of distributed computing in analytics is the Hadoop ecosystem, which includes distributed file storage via Hadoop Distributed File System (HDFS), processing via MapReduce, data analysis via Pig, and more. Apache Spark is another popular distributed processing framework, which is quickly surpassing Hadoop in popularity.

Though not all data pipelines require the use of distributed computing, data engineers need to know how and when to utilize such a framework.

Basic System Administration

A data engineer is expected to be proficient on the Linux command line and be able to perform tasks such as analyze application logs, schedule cron jobs, and troubleshoot firewall and other security settings. Even when working fully on a cloud provider such as AWS, Azure, or Google Cloud, they'll end up using those skills to get cloud services working together and data pipelines deployed.

A Goal-Oriented Mentality

A good data engineer doesn't just possess technical skills. They may not interface with stakeholders on a regular basis, but the analysts and data scientists on the team certainly will. The data engineer will make better architectural decisions if they're aware of the reason they're building a pipeline in the first place.

Why Build Data Pipelines?

In the same way that the tip of the iceberg is all that can be seen by a passing ship, the end product of the analytics workflow is all that the majority of an organization sees. Executives see dashboards and pristine charts. Marketing shares cleanly packaged insights on social media. Customer support optimizes the call center staffing based on the output of a predictive demand model.

What most people outside of analytics often fail to appreciate is that to generate what is seen, there's a complex machinery that is unseen. For every dashboard and insight that a data analyst generates and for each predictive model developed by a data scientist, there are data pipelines working behind the scenes. It's not uncommon for a single dashboard, or even a single metric, to be derived from data originating in multiple source systems. In addition, data pipelines do more than just extract data from sources and load them into simple database tables or flat files for analysts to use. Raw data is refined along the way to clean, structure, normalize, combine, aggregate, and at times anonymize or otherwise secure it. In other words, there's a lot more going on below the water line.

Supplying Data to Analysts and Data Scientists

Don't rely on data analysts and data scientists hunting for and procuring data on their own for each project that comes their way. The risks of acting on stale data, multiple sources of truth, and bogging down analytics talent in data acquisition are too great. Data pipelines ensure that the proper data is delivered so the rest of the analytics organization can focus their time on what they do best: delivering insights.

How Are Pipelines Built?

Along with data engineers, numerous tools to build and support data pipelines have emerged in recent years. Some are open source, some commercial, and some are homegrown. Some pipelines are written in Python, some in Java, some in another language, and some with no code at all.

Throughout this Pocket Reference I explore some of the most popular products and frameworks for building pipelines, as well as discuss how to determine which to use based on your organization's needs and constraints.

Though I do not cover all such products in depth, I do provide examples and sample code for some. All code in this book is written in Python and SQL. These are the most common, and in my opinion, the most accessible, languages for building data pipelines.

In addition, pipelines are not just built—they are monitored, maintained, and extended. Data engineers are tasked with not just delivering data once, but building pipelines and supporting infrastructure that deliver and process it reliably, securely, and on time. It's no small feat, but when it's done well, the value of an organization's data can truly be unlocked.

## CHAPTER 2

A Modern Data Infrastructure

Before deciding on products and design for building pipelines, it's worth understanding what makes up a modern data stack. As with most things in technology, there's no single right way to design your analytics ecosystem or choose products and vendors. Regardless, there are some key needs and concepts that have become industry standard and set the stage for best practices in implementing pipelines.

Let's take a look at the key components of such an infrastructure as displayed in Figure 2-1. Future chapters explore how each component factors into the design and implementation of data pipelines.

Diversity of Data Sources

The majority of organizations have dozens, if not hundreds, of data sources that feed their analytics endeavors. Data sources vary across many dimensions covered in this section.

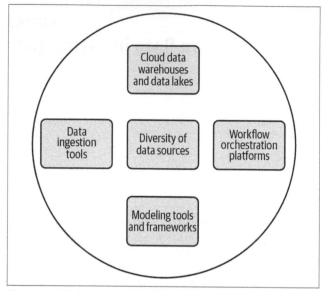

Figure 2-1. The key components of a modern data infrastructure.

Source System Ownership

It's typical for an analytics team to ingest data from source systems that are built and owned by the organization as well as from third-party tools and vendors. For example, an ecommerce company might store data from their shopping cart in a PostgreSQL (also known as Postgres) database behind their web app. They may also use a third-party web analytics tool such as Google Analytics to track usage on their website. The combination of the two data sources (illustrated in Figure 2-2) is required to get a full understanding of customer behavior leading up to a purchase. Thus, a data pipeline that ends with an analysis of such behavior starts with the ingestion of data from both sources.

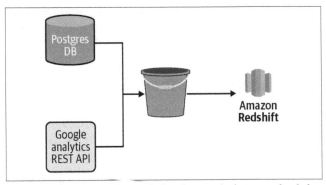

Figure 2-2. A simple pipeline with data from multiple sources loaded into an S3 bucket and then a Redshift database.

NOTE

The term *data ingestion* refers to extracting data from one source and loading it into another.

Understanding the ownership of source systems is important for several reasons. First, for third-party data sources you're likely limited as to what data you can access and how you can access it. Most vendors make a REST API available, but few will give you direct access to your data in the form of a SQL database. Even fewer will give you much in the way of customization of what data you can access and at what level of granularity.

Internally built systems present the analytics team with more opportunities to customize the data available as well as the method of access. However, they present other challenges as well. Were the systems built with consideration of data ingestion? Often the answer is no, which has implications ranging from the ingestion putting unintended load on the system to the inability to load data incrementally. If you're lucky, the engineering team that owns the source system will have the time and willingness to work with you, but in the reality of resource constraints, you may find it's not dissimilar to working with an external vendor.

Ingestion Interface and Data Structure

Regardless of who owns the source data, how you get it and in what form is the first thing a data engineer will examine when building a new data ingestion. First, what is the interface to the data? Some of the most common include the following:

- A database behind an application, such as a Postgres or MySQL database
- A layer of abstraction on top of a system such as a REST API
- A stream processing platform such as Apache Kafka
- A shared network file system or cloud storage bucket containing logs, comma-separated value (CSV) files, and other flat files
- A data warehouse or data lake
- Data in HDFS or HBase database

In addition to the interface, the structure of the data will vary. Here are some common examples:

- JSON from a REST API
- Well-structured data from a MySQL database
- JSON within columns of a MySQL database table
- Semistructured log data
- CSV, fixed-width format (FWF), and other flat file formats
- JSON in flat files
- Stream output from Kafka

Each interface and data structure presents its own challenges and opportunities. Well-structured data is often easiest to work with, but it's usually structured in the interest of an application or website. Beyond the ingestion of the data, further steps in the pipeline will likely be necessary to clean and transform into a structure better suited for an analytics project.

Semistructured data such as JSON is increasingly common and has the advantage of the structure of attribute-value pairs and nesting of objects. However, unlike a relational database, there is no guarantee that each object in the same dataset will have the same structure. As you'll see later in this book, how one deals with missing or incomplete data in a pipeline is context dependent and increasingly necessary as the rigidity of the structure in data is reduced.

Unstructured data is common for some analytics endeavors. For example, Natural Language Processing (NLP) models require vast amounts of free text data to train and validate. Computer Vision (CV) projects require images and video content. Even less daunting projects such as scraping data from web pages have a need for free text data from the web in addition to the semistructured HTML markup of a web page.

Data Volume

Though data engineers and hiring managers alike enjoy bragging about petabyte-scale datasets, the reality is that most organizations value small datasets as much as large ones. In addition, it's common to ingest and model small and large datasets in tandem. Though the design decisions at each step in a pipeline must take data volume into consideration, high volume does not mean high value.

All that said, most organizations have at least one dataset that is key to both analytical needs as well as high volume. What's *high volume*? There's no easy definition, but as it pertains to pipelines, it's best to think in terms of a spectrum rather than a binary definition of *high-* and *low-* volume datasets.

Data Cleanliness and Validity

Just as there is great diversity in data sources, the quality of source data varies greatly. As the old saying goes, "garbage in, garbage out." It's important to understand the limitations and deficiencies of source data and address them in the appropriate sections of your pipelines.

There are many common characteristics of "messy data," including, but not limited to, the following:

- Duplicate or ambiguous records
- Orphaned records
- Incomplete or missing records
- Text encoding errors
- Inconsistent formats (for example, phone numbers with or without dashes)
- Mislabeled or unlabeled data

Of course, there are numerous others, as well as data validity issues specific to the context of the source system.

There's no magic bullet for ensuring data cleanliness and validity, but in a modern data ecosystem, there are key characteristics and approaches that we'll see throughout this book:

Assume the worst, expect the best

Pristine datasets only exist in academic literature. Assume your input datasets will contain numerous validity and consistency issues, but build pipelines that identify and cleanse data in the interest of clean output.

Clean and validate data in the system best suited to do so

There are times when it's better to wait to clean data until later in a pipeline. For example, modern pipelines tend to follow an extract-load-transform (ELT) rather than extract-transform-load (ETL) approach for data warehousing (more in Chapter 3). It's sometimes optimal to load data into a data lake in a fairly raw form and to worry about structuring and cleaning later in the pipeline. In other words, use the right tool for the right job rather than rushing the cleaning and validation processes.

Validate often

Even if you don't clean up data early in a pipeline, don't wait until the end of the pipeline to validate it. You'll have a much harder time determining where things went wrong. Conversely, don't validate once early in a pipeline and assume all will go well in subsequent steps. Chapter 8 digs deeper into validation.

Latency and Bandwidth of the Source System

The need to frequently extract high volumes of data from source systems is a common use case in a modern data stack. Doing so presents challenges, however. Data extraction steps in pipelines must contend with API rate limits, connection timeouts, slow downloads, and source system owners who are unhappy due to strain placed on their systems.

NOTE

As I'll discuss in Chapters 4 and 5 in more detail, data ingestion is the first step in most data pipelines. Understanding the characteristics of source systems and their data is thus the first step in designing pipelines and making decisions regarding infrastructure further downstream.

Cloud Data Warehouses and Data Lakes

Three things transformed the landscape of analytics and data warehousing over the last 10 years, and they're all related to the emergence of the major public cloud providers (Amazon, Google, and Microsoft):

- The ease of building and deploying data pipelines, data lakes, warehouses, and analytics processing in the cloud. No more waiting on IT departments and budget approval for large up-front costs. Managed services—databases in particular—have become mainstream.

- Continued drop-in storage costs in the cloud.

- The emergence of highly scalable, columnar databases, such as Amazon Redshift, Snowflake, and Google Big Query.

These changes breathed new life into data warehouses and introduced the concept of a data lake. Though Chapter 5 covers data warehouses and data lakes in more detail, it's worth briefly defining both now, in order to clarify their place in a modern data ecosystem.

A *data warehouse* is a database where data from different systems is stored and modeled to support analysis and other activities related to answering questions with it. Data in a data warehouse is structured and optimized for reporting and analysis queries.

A *data lake* is where data is stored, but without the structure or query optimization of a data warehouse. It will likely contain a high volume of data as well as a variety of data types. For example, a single data lake might contain a collection of blog posts stored as text files, flat file extracts from a relational database, and JSON objects containing events generated by sensors in an industrial system. It can even store structured data like a standard database, though it's not optimized for querying such data in the interest of reporting and analysis.

There is a place for both data warehouses and data lakes in the same data ecosystem, and data pipelines often move data between both.

Data Ingestion Tools

The need to ingest data from one system to another is common to nearly all data pipelines. As previously discussed in this chapter, data teams must contend with a diversity of data sources from which to ingest data from. Thankfully, a number of commercial and open source tools are available in a modern data infrastructure.

In this Pocket Reference, I discuss some of the most common of these tools and frameworks, including:

- Singer
- Stitch
- Fivetran

Despite the prevalence of these tools, some teams decide to build custom code to ingest data. Some even develop their own frameworks. The reasons vary by organization but are often related to cost, a culture of building over buying, and concerns about the legal and security risks of trusting an external vendor. In Chapter 5, I discuss the build versus buy trade-offs that are unique to data ingestion tools. Of particular interest is whether the value of a commercial solution is to make it easier for data engineers to build data ingestions into their pipelines or to enable nondata engineers (such as data analysts) to build ingestions themselves.

As Chapters 4 and 5 discuss, data ingestion is traditionally both the *extract* and *load* steps of an ETL or ELT process. Some tools focus on just these steps, while others provide the user with some *transform* capabilities as well. In practice, I find most data teams choose to limit the number of transformations they make during data ingestion and thus stick to ingestion tools that are good at two things: extracting data from a source and loading it into a destination.

Data Transformation and Modeling Tools

Though the bulk of this chapter has focused on moving data between sources and destinations (data ingestion), there is much more to data pipelines and the movement of data. Pipelines are also made up of tasks that transform and model data for new purposes, such as machine learning, analysis, and reporting.

The terms *data modeling* and *data transformation* are often used interchangeably; however, for the purposes of this text, I will differentiate between them:

Data transformation
> Transforming data is a broad term that is signified by the *T* in an ETL or ELT process. A transformation can be something as simple as converting a timestamp stored in a table from one time zone to another. It can also be a more complex operation that creates a new metric from multiple source columns that are aggregated and filtered through some business logic.

Data modeling
> Data modeling is a more specific type of data transformation. A data model structures and defines data in a format that is understood and optimized for data analysis. A data model is usually represented as one or more tables in a data warehouse. The process of creating data models is discussed in more detail in Chapter 6.

Like data ingestion, there are a number of methodologies and tools that are present in a modern data infrastructure. As previously noted, some data ingestion tools provide some level of data transformation capabilities, but these are often quite simple. For example, for the sake of protecting *personally identifiable information* (*PII*) it may be desirable to turn an email address into a hashed value that is stored in the final destination. Such a transformation is usually performed during the ingestion process.

For more complex data transformations and data modeling, I find it desirable to seek out tools and frameworks specifically designed for the task, such as dbt (see Chapter 9). In addition, data transformation is often context-specific and can be written in a language familiar to data engineers and data analysts, such as SQL or Python.

Data models that will be used for analysis and reporting are typically defined and written in SQL or via point-and-click user interfaces. Just like build-versus-buy trade-offs, there are considerations in choosing to build models using SQL versus a *no-code* tool. SQL is a highly accessible language that is common to both data engineers and analysts. It empowers the analyst to work directly with the data and optimize the design of models for their needs. It's also used in nearly every organization, thus providing a familiar entry point for new hires to a team. In most cases, choosing a transformation framework that supports building data models in SQL rather than via a point-and-click user interface is desirable. You'll get far more customizability and own your development process from end to end.

Chapter 6 discusses transforming and modeling data at length.

Workflow Orchestration Platforms

As the complexity and number of data pipelines in an organization grows, it's important to introduce a *workflow orchestration platform* to your data infrastructure. These platforms manage the scheduling and flow of tasks in a pipeline. Imagine a pipeline with a dozen tasks ranging from data ingestions written in Python to data transformations written in SQL that must run in a particular sequence throughout the day. It's not a simple challenge to schedule and manage dependencies between each task. Every data team faces this challenge, but thankfully there are numerous workflow orchestration platforms available to alleviate the pain.

Workflow orchestration platforms are also referred to as *workflow management systems* (WMSs), *orchestration platforms*, or *orchestration frameworks*. I use these terms interchangeably in this text.

Some platforms, such as Apache Airflow, Luigi, and AWS Glue, are designed for more general use cases and are thus used for a wide variety of data pipelines. Others, such as Kubeflow Pipelines, are designed for more specific use cases and platforms (machine learning workflows built on Docker containers in the case of Kubeflow Pipelines).

Directed Acyclic Graphs

Nearly all modern orchestration frameworks represent the flow and dependencies of tasks in a pipeline as a graph. However, pipeline graphs have some specific constraints.

Pipeline steps are always *directed*, meaning they start with a general task or multiple tasks and end with a specific task or tasks. This is required to guarantee a path of execution. In other words, it ensures that tasks do not run before all their dependent tasks are completed successfully.

Pipeline graphs must also be *acyclic*, meaning that a task cannot point back to a previously completed task. In other words, it cannot cycle back. If it could, then a pipeline could run endlessly!

With these two constraints in mind, orchestration pipelines produce graphs called directed acyclic graphs (DaGs). Figure 2-3 illustrates a simple DAG. In this example, Task A must complete before Tasks B and C can start. Once they are both completed, then Task D can start. Once Task D is complete, the pipeline is completed as well.

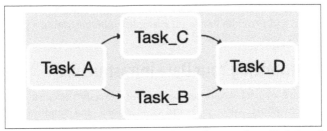

Figure 2-3. A DAG with four tasks. After Task A completes, Task B and Task C run. When they both complete, Task D runs.

DAGs are a representation of a set of tasks and not where the logic of the tasks is defined. An orchestration platform is capable of running tasks of all sorts.

For example, consider a data pipeline with three tasks. It is represented as a DAG in Figure 2-4.

- The first executes a SQL script that queries data from a relational database and stores the result in a CSV file.
- The second runs a Python script that loads the CSV file, cleans, and then reshapes the data before saving a new version of the file.
- Finally, a third task, which runs the COPY command in SQL, loads the CSV created by the second task into a Snowflake data warehouse.

Figure 2-4. A DAG with three tasks that run in sequence to extract data from a SQL database, clean and reshape the data using a Python script, and then load the resulting data into a data warehouse.

The orchestration platform executes each task, but the logic of the tasks exists as SQL and Python code, which runs on different systems across the data infrastructure.

Chapter 7 discusses workflow orchestration platforms in more detail and provides hands-on examples of orchestrating a pipeline in Apache Airflow.

Customizing Your Data Infrastructure

It's rare to find two organizations with exactly the same data infrastructure. Most pick and choose tools and vendors that meet their specific needs and build the rest on their own. Though I talk in detail about some of the most popular tools and products throughout this book, many more come to market each year.

As previously noted, depending on the culture and resources in your organization, you may be encouraged to build most of your data infrastructure on your own, or to rely on SaaS vendors instead. Regardless of which way you lean on the build-versus-buy scale, you can build the high-quality data infrastructure necessary to build high-quality data pipelines.

What's important is understanding your constraints (dollars, engineering resources, security, and legal risk tolerance) and the resulting trade-offs. I speak to these throughout the text and call out key decision points in selecting a product or tool.

CHAPTER 3

Common Data Pipeline Patterns

Even for seasoned data engineers, designing a new data pipeline is a new journey each time. As discussed in Chapter 2, differing data sources and infrastructure present both challenges and opportunities. In addition, pipelines are built with different goals and constraints. Must the data be processed in near real time? Can it be updated daily? Will it be modeled for use in a dashboard or as input to a machine learning model?

Thankfully, there are some common patterns in data pipelines that have proven successful and are extensible to many use cases. In this chapter, I will define these patterns. Subsequent chapters implement pipelines built on them.

ETL and ELT

There is perhaps no pattern more well known than ETL and its more modern sibling, ELT. Both are patterns widely used in data warehousing and business intelligence. In more recent years, they've inspired pipeline patterns for data science and machine learning models running in production. They are so well known that many people use these terms synonymously with data pipelines rather than patterns that many pipelines follow.

Given their roots in data warehousing, it's easiest to describe them in that context, which is what this section does. Later sections in this chapter describe how they are used for particular use cases.

Both patterns are approaches to data processing used to feed data into a data warehouse and make it useful to analysts and reporting tools. The difference between the two is the order of their final two steps (transform and load), but the design implications in choosing between them are substantial, as I'll explain throughout this chapter. First, let's explore the steps of ETL and ELT.

The *extract* step gathers data from various sources in preparation for loading and transforming. Chapter 2 discussed the diversity of these sources and methods of extraction.

The *load* step brings either the raw data (in the case of ELT) or the fully transformed data (in the case of ETL) into the final destination. Either way, the end result is loading data into the data warehouse, data lake, or other destination.

The *transform* step is where the raw data from each source system is combined and formatted in a such a way that it's useful to analysts, visualization tools, or whatever use case your pipeline is serving. There's a lot to this step, regardless of whether you design your process as ETL or ELT, all of which is explored in detail in Chapter 6.

Separation of Extract and Load

The combination of the extraction and loading steps is often referred to as *data ingestion*. Especially in ELT and the EtLT subpattern (note the lowercase *t*), which is defined later in this chapter, extraction and loading capabilities are often tightly coupled and packaged together in software frameworks. When designing pipelines, however, it is still best to consider the two steps as separate due to the complexity of coordinating extracts and loads across different systems and infrastructure.

> Chapters 4 and 5 describe data ingestion techniques in more detail and provide implementation examples using common frameworks.

The Emergence of ELT over ETL

ETL was the gold standard of data pipeline patterns for decades. Though it's still used, more recently ELT has emerged as the pattern of choice. Why? Prior to the modern breed of data warehouses, primarily in the cloud (see Chapter 2), data teams didn't have access to data warehouses with the storage or compute necessary to handle loading vast amounts of raw data and transforming it into usable data models all in the same place. In addition, data warehouses at the time were row-based databases that worked well for transactional use cases, but not for the high-volume, bulk queries that are commonplace in analytics. Thus, data was first extracted from source systems and then transformed on a separate system before being loaded into a warehouse for any final data modeling and querying by analysts and visualization tools.

The majority of today's data warehouses are built on highly scalable, columnar databases that can both store and run bulk transforms on large datasets in a cost-effective manner. Thanks to the I/O efficiency of a columnar database, data compression, and the ability to distribute data and queries across many nodes that can work together to process data, things have changed. It's now better to focus on extracting data and loading it into a data warehouse where you can then perform the necessary transformations to complete the pipeline.

The impact of the difference between row-based and column-based data warehouses cannot be overstated. Figure 3-1 illustrates an example of how records are stored on disk in a row-based database, such as MySQL or Postgres. Each row of the database is stored together on disk, in one or more blocks depending on the size of each record. If a record is smaller than a single block or not cleanly divisible by the block size, it leaves some disk space unused.

OrderId	CustomerId	ShippingCountry	OrderTotal
1	1258	US	55.25
2	5698	AUS	125.36
3	2265	US	776.95
4	8954	CA	32.16

Block 1	1, 1258, US, 55.25
Block 2	2, 5698, AUS, 125.36
Block 3	3, 2265, US, 776.95
Block 4	4, 8954, CA, 32.16

Figure 3-1. A table stored in a row-based storage database. Each block contains a record (row) from the table.

Consider an online transaction processing (OLTP) database use case such as an e-commerce web application that leverages a MySQL database for storage. The web app requests reads and writes from and to the MySQL database, often involving multiple values from each record, such as the details of an order on an order confirmation page. It's also likely to query or update only one order at a time. Therefore, row-based storage is optimal since the data the application needs is stored in close proximity on disk, and the amount of data queried at one time is small.

The inefficient use of disk space due to records leaving empty space in blocks is a reasonable trade-off in this case, as the speed to reading and writing single records frequently is what's most important. However, in analytics the situation is reversed. Instead of the need to read and write small amounts of data frequently, we often read and write a large amount of data infrequently. In addition, it's less likely that an analytical query requires many, or all, of the columns in a table but rather a single column of a table with many columns.

For example, consider the order table in our fictional e-commerce application. Among other things, it contains the dollar amount of the order as well as the country it's shipping to. Unlike the web application, which works with orders one at a time, an analyst using the data warehouse will want to analyze orders in bulk. In addition, the table containing order data in the data warehouse has additional columns that contain values from multiple tables in our MySQL database. For example, it might contain the information about the customer who placed the order. Perhaps the analyst wants to sum up all orders placed by customers with currently active accounts. Such a query might involve millions of records, but only read from two columns, OrderTotal and CustomerActive. After all, analytics is not about creating or changing data (like in OLTP) but rather the derivation of metrics and the understanding of data.

As illustrated in Figure 3-2, a columnar database, such as Snowflake or Amazon Redshift, stores data in disk blocks by column rather than row. In our use case, the query written by the analyst only needs to access blocks that store OrderTotal and CustomerActive values rather than blocks that store the row-based records such as the MySQL database. Thus, there's less disk I/O as well as less data to load into memory to perform the filtering and summing required by the analyst's query. A final benefit is reduction in storage, thanks to the fact that blocks can be fully utilized and optimally compressed since the same data type is stored in each block rather than multiple types that tend to occur in a single row-based record.

All in all, the emergence of columnar databases means that storing, transforming, and querying large datasets is efficient within a data warehouse. Data engineers can use that to their advantage by building pipeline steps that specialize in extracting and loading data into warehouses where it can be transformed, modeled, and queried by analysts and data scientists who are more comfortable within the confines of a database. As such, ELT has taken over as the ideal pattern for data warehouse pipelines as well as other use cases in machine learning and data product development.

OrderId	CustomerId	Shipping Country	Order Total	Customer Active
1	1258	US	55.25	TRUE
2	5698	AUS	125.36	TRUE
3	2265	US	776.95	TRUE
4	8954	CA	32.16	FALSE

Block 1	1, 2, 3, 4
Block 2	1258, 5698, 2265, 8954
Block 3	US, AUS, US, CA
Block 4	55.25, 125.36, 776.95. 32.16
Block 5	TRUE, TRUE, TRUE, FALSE

Figure 3-2. A table stored in a column-based storage database. Each disk block contains data from the same column. The two columns involved in our example query are highlighted. Only these blocks must be accessed to run the query. Each block contains data of the same type, making compression optimal.

EtLT Subpattern

When ELT emerged as the dominant pattern, it became clear that doing some transformation after extraction, but before loading, was still beneficial. However, instead of transformation involving business logic or data modeling, this type of transformation is more limited in scope. I refer to this as *lowercase t* transformation, or *EtLT*.

Some examples of the type of transformation that fits into the EtLT subpattern include the following:

- Deduplicate records in a table
- Parse URL parameters into individual components

- Mask or otherwise obfuscate sensitive data

These types of transforms are either fully disconnected from business logic or, in the case of something like masking sensitive data, at times required as early in a pipeline as possible for legal or security reasons. In addition, there is value in using the right tool for the right job. As Chapters 4 and 5 illustrate in greater detail, most modern data warehouses load data most efficiently if it's prepared well. In pipelines moving a high volume of data, or where latency is key, performing some basic transforms between the extract and load steps is worth the effort.

You can assume that the remaining ELT-related patterns are designed to include the EtLT subpattern as well.

ELT for Data Analysis

ELT has become the most common and, in my opinion, most optimal pattern for pipelines built for data analysis. As already discussed, columnar databases are well suited to handling high volumes of data. They are also designed to handle wide tables, meaning tables with many columns, thanks to the fact that only data in columns used in a given query are scanned on disk and loaded into memory.

Beyond technical considerations, data analysts are typically fluent in SQL. With ELT, data engineers can focus on the extract and load steps in a pipeline (data ingestion), while analysts can utilize SQL to transform the data that's been ingested as needed for reporting and analysis. Such a clean separation is not possible with an ETL pattern, as data engineers are needed across the entire pipeline. As shown in Figure 3-3, ELT allows data team members to focus on their strengths with less interdependencies and coordination.

In addition, the ELT pattern reduces the need to predict exactly what analysts will do with the data at the time of building extract and load processes. Though understanding the general use case is required to extract and load the proper data, saving the transform step for later gives analysts more options and flexibility.

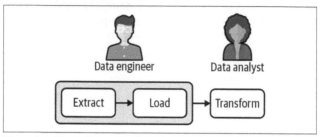

Figure 3-3. The ELT pattern allows for a clean split of responsibilities between data engineers and data analysts (or data scientists). Each role can work autonomously with the tools and languages they are comfortable in.

NOTE

With the emergence of ELT, data analysts have become more autonomous and empowered to deliver value from data without being "blocked" by data engineers. Data engineers can focus on data ingestion and supporting infrastructure that enables analysts to write and deploy their own transform code written as SQL. With that empowerment have come new job titles such as the *analytics engineer*. Chapter 6 discusses how these data analysts and analytics engineers transform data to build data models.

ELT for Data Science

Data pipelines built for data science teams are similar to those built for data analysis in a data warehouse. Like the analysis use case, data engineers are focused on ingesting data into a data warehouse or data lake. However, data scientists have different needs from the data than data analysts do.

Though data science is a broad field, in general, data scientists will need access to more granular—and at times raw—data than data analysts do. While data analysts build data models that produce metrics and power dashboards, data scientists spend their days exploring data and building predictive models. While the details of the role of a data scientist are out of the scope of this book, this high-level distinction matters to the design of pipelines serving data scientists.

If you're building pipelines to support data scientists, you'll find that the extract and load steps of the ELT pattern will remain pretty much the same as they will for supporting analytics. Chapters 4 and 5 outline those steps in technical detail. Data scientists might also benefit from working with some of the data models built for analysts in the transform step of an ELT pipeline (Chapter 6), but they'll likely branch off and use much of the data acquired during extract-load.

ELT for Data Products and Machine Learning

Data is used for more than analysis, reporting, and predictive models. It's also used for powering *data products*. Some common examples of data products include the following:

- A content recommendation engine that powers a video streaming home screen
- A personalized search engine on an e-commerce website
- An application that performs sentiment analysis on user-generated restaurant reviews

Each of those data products is likely powered by one or more machine learning (ML) models, which are hungry for training and validation data. Such data may come from a variety of source systems and undergo some level of transformation to prepare it for use in the model. An ELT-like pattern is well suited for such needs, though there are a number of specific challenges in all steps of a pipeline that's designed for a data product.

Steps in a Machine Learning Pipeline

Like pipelines built for analysis, which this book is primarily focused on, pipelines built for ML follow a pattern similar to ELT—at least in the beginning of the pipeline. The difference is that instead of the transform step focusing on transforming data into data models, once data is extracted and loaded into a warehouse or data lake, there a several steps involved in building and updating the ML model.

If you're familiar with ML development, these steps may look familiar as well:

Data ingestion

This step follows the same process that I outline in Chapters 4 and 5. Though the data you ingest may differ, the logic remains primarily the same for pipelines built for analytics as well as ML, but with one additional consideration for ML pipelines. That is, ensuring that the data you ingest is versioned in a way that ML models can later refer to as a specific dataset for training or validation. There are a number of tools and approaches for versioning datasets. I suggest referring to "Further Reading on ML Pipelines" on page 32 to learn more.

Data preprocessing

The data that's ingested is unlikely to be ready to use in ML development. Preprocessing is where data is cleaned and otherwise prepared for models. For example, this is the step in a pipeline where text is tokenized, features are converted to numerical values, and input values are normalized.

Model training

After new data is ingested and preprocessed, ML models need to be retrained.

Model deployment

Deploying models to production can be the most challenging part of going from research-oriented machine learning to a true data product. Here, not only is versioning of datasets necessary, but versioning of trained models is also needed. Often, a REST API is used to allow for querying of a deployed model, and API endpoints for various versions of a model will be used. It's a lot to keep track of and takes coordination between data scientists, machine learning engineers, and data engineers to get to a production state. A well-designed pipeline is key to gluing it together.

Validating Ingested Data

As Chapter 8 discusses, validating data in a pipeline is essential and has a place throughout pipelines. In pipelines built for data analysts, validation often happens after data ingestion (extract-load) as well as after data modeling (transform). In ML pipelines, validation of the data that's ingested is also important. Don't confuse this critical step with validation of the ML model itself, which is of course a standard part of ML development.

Incorporate Feedback in the Pipeline

Any good ML pipeline will also include gathering feedback for improving the model. Take the example of a content recommendation model for a video streaming service. To measure and improve the model in the future, you'll need to keep track of what it recommends to users, what recommendations they click, and what recommended content they enjoy after they click it. To do so, you'll need to work with the development team leveraging the model on the streaming services home screen. They'll need to implement some type of event collection that keeps track of each recommendation made to each user; the version of the model that recommended it; and when it's clicked; and then carry that click-through to the data they're likely already collecting related to a user's content consumption.

All that information can then be ingested back into the data warehouse and incorporated into future versions of the model, either as training data or to be analyzed and considered by a human (a data scientist perhaps) for inclusion in a future model or experiment.

In addition, the data collected can be ingested, transformed, and analyzed by data analysts in the ELT pattern described throughout this book. Analysts will often be tasked with measuring the effectiveness of models and building dashboards to display key metrics of the model to the organization. Stakeholders can use such dashboards to make sense of how effective various models are to the business and to their customers.

Further Reading on ML Pipelines

Building pipelines for machine learning models is a robust topic. Depending on your infrastructure choices and the complexity of your ML environment, there are several books I recommend for further learning:

> *Building Machine Learning Pipelines* by Hannes Hapke and Catherine Nelson (O'Reilly, 2020)
> *Machine Learning with Scikit-Learn, Keras, and Tensor-Flow*, 2nd edition, by Aurélien Géron (O'Reilly, 2019)

In addition, the following book is a highly accessible introduction to machine learning:

> *Introduction to Machine Learning with Python* by Andreas C. Müller and Sarah Guido (O'Reilly, 2016)

## CHAPTER 4

Data Ingestion: Extracting Data

As discussed in Chapter 3, the ELT pattern is the ideal design for data pipelines built for data analysis, data science, and data products. The first two steps in the ELT pattern, extract and load, are collectively referred to as *data ingestion*. This chapter discusses getting your development environment and infrastructure set up for both, and it goes through the specifics of extracting data from various source systems. Chapter 5 discusses loading the resulting datasets into a data warehouse.

NOTE

The extract and load code samples in this chapter are fully decoupled from each other. Coordinating the two steps to complete a data ingestion is a topic that's discussed in Chapter 7.

As discussed in Chapter 2, there are numerous types of source systems to extract from, as well as numerous destinations to load into. In addition, data comes in many forms, all of which present different challenges for ingesting it.

This chapter and the next include code samples for exporting and ingesting data from and to common systems. The code is highly simplified and contains only minimal error handing. Each example is intended as an easy-to-understand starting point for data ingestions, but is fully functional and extendable to more scalable solutions.

NOTE

The code samples in this chapter write extracted data to CSV files to be loaded into the destination data warehouse. There are times when it makes more sense to store extracted data in another format, such as JSON, prior to loading. Where applicable, I note where you might want to consider making such an adjustment.

Chapter 5 also discusses some open source frameworks you can build off of, and commercial alternatives that give data engineers and analysts "low code" options for ingesting data.

Setting Up Your Python Environment

All code samples that follow are written in Python and SQL and use open source frameworks that are common in the data engineering field today. For simplicity, the number of sources and destinations is limited. However, where applicable, I provide notes on how to modify for similar systems.

To run the sample code, you'll need a physical or virtual machine running Python 3.x. You'll also need to install and import a few libraries.

If you don't have Python installed on your machine, you can get the distribution and installer for your OS directly from them (*https://oreil.ly/ytH4s*).

Before you install the libraries used in this chapter, it's best to create a *virtual environment* to install them into. To do so, you can use a tool called virtualenv. virtualenv is helpful in managing Python libraries for different projects and applications. It allows you to install Python libraries within a scope specific to your project rather than globally. First, create a virtual environment named *env*.

```
$ python -m venv env
```

Now that your virtual environment is created, activate it with the following command:

```
$ source env/bin/activate
```

You can verify that your virtual environment is activated in two ways. First, you'll notice that your command prompt is now prefixed by the environment name:

```
(env) $
```

You can also use the which python command to verify where Python is looking for libraries. You should see something like this, which shows the path of the virtual environment directory:

```
(env) $ which python
env/bin/python
```

Now it's safe to install the libraries you need for the code samples that follow.

Throughout this chapter, you'll use `pip` to install the libraries used in the code samples. `pip` (*https://pypi.org/project/pip*) is a tool that ships with most Python distributions.

The first library you'll install using `pip` is `configparser`, which will be used to read configuration information you'll add to a file later.

```
(env) $ pip install configparser
```

Next, create a file named *pipeline.conf* in the same directory as the Python scripts you'll create in the following sections. Leave the file empty for now. The code samples in this chapter will call for adding to it. In Linux and Mac operating systems, you can create the empty file on the command line with the following command:

```
(env) $ touch pipeline.conf
```

Don't Add Your Config Files to a Git Repo!

Because you'll be storing credentials and connection information in the configuration file, make sure you don't add it to your Git repo. This information should only be stored locally and on systems that are secure and authorized to access your S3 bucket, source systems, and data warehouse. The safest way to ensure exclusion in the repo is to give your config files an extension like *.conf* and add a line to your *.gitignore* file with **.conf*.

Setting Up Cloud File Storage

For each example in this chapter, you'll be using an Amazon Simple Storage Service (Amazon S3 or simply S3) bucket for file storage. S3 is hosted on AWS, and as the name implies, S3 is a simple way to store and access files. It's also very cost effective. As of this writing, AWS offers 5 GB of free S3 storage for 12 months with a new AWS account and charges less than 3 cents USD per month per gigabyte for the standard S3 class of storage after that. Given the simplicity of the samples in this chapter, you'll be able to store the necessary data in S3 for free if you are still in the first 12 months of creating an AWS account, or for less than a $1 a month after that.

To run the samples in this chapter, you'll need an S3 bucket. Thankfully, creating an S3 bucket is simple, and the latest instructions can be found in the AWS documentation (*https://oreil.ly/7W9ZD*). Setting up the proper access control to the S3 bucket is dependent upon which data warehouse you are using. In general, it's best to use AWS Identity and Access Management (IAM) roles for access management policies. Detailed instructions for setting up such access for both an Amazon Redshift and Snowflake data warehouse are in the sections that follow, but for now, follow the instruction to create a new bucket. Name it whatever you'd like; I suggest using the default settings, including keeping the bucket private.

Each extraction example extracts data from the given source system and stores the output in the S3 bucket. Each loading example in Chapter 5 loads that data from the S3 bucket into the destination. This is a common pattern in data pipelines. Every major public cloud provider has a service similar to S3. Equivalents on other public clouds are Azure Storage in Microsoft Azure and Google Cloud Storage (GCS) in GCP.

It's also possible to modify each example to use local or on-premises storage. However, there is additional work required to load data into your data warehouse from storage outside of its specific cloud provider. Regardless, the patterns described in this chapter are valid no matter which cloud provider you use, or if you choose to host your data infrastructure on-premises.

Before I move on to each example, there's one more Python library that you'll need to install so that your scripts for extracting and loading can interact with your S3 bucket. Boto3 is the AWS SDK for Python. Make sure the virtual environment you set up in the previous section is active and use pip to install it:

```
(env) $ pip install boto3
```

In the examples that follow, you'll be asked to import boto3 into your Python scripts like this:

```
import boto3
```

Because you'll be using the boto3 Python library to interact with your S3 bucket, you'll also need to create an IAM user, generate access keys for that user, and store the keys in a configuration file that your Python scripts can read from. This is all necessary so that your scripts have permissions to read and write files in your S3 bucket.

First, create the IAM user:

1. Under the Services menu in the AWS console (or top nav bar), navigate to IAM.

2. In the navigation pane, click Users and then click "Add user." Type the username for the new user. In this example, name the user *data_pipeline_readwrite*.

3. Click the type of access for this IAM user. Click "programmatic access" since this user won't need to log into the AWS Console, but rather access AWS resources programmatically via Python scripts.

4. Click Next: Permissions.

5. On the "Set permissions" page, click the "Attach existing policies to user directly" option. Add the AmazonS3FullAccess policy.

6. Click Next: Tags. It's a best practice in AWS to add tags to various objects and services so you can find them later. This is optional, however.

7. Click Next: Review to verify your settings. If everything looks good, click "Create user."

8. You'll want to save the access key ID and secret access key for the new IAM user. To do so, click Download.csv and then save the file to a safe location so you can use it in just a moment.

Finally, add a section to the *pipeline.conf* file called [aws_boto_credentials] to store the credentials for the IAM user and the S3 bucket information. You can find your AWS account ID by clicking your account name at the top right of any page when logged into the AWS site. Use the name of the S3 bucket you created earlier for the bucket_name value. The new section in *pipline.conf* will look like this:

```
[aws_boto_credentials]
access_key = ijfiojr54rg8er8erg8erg8
secret_key = 5r4f84er4ghrg484eg84re84ger84
bucket_name = pipeline-bucket
account_id = 4515465518
```

Extracting Data from a MySQL Database

Extracting data from a MySQL database can be done in two ways:

- Full or incremental extraction using SQL
- Binary Log (binlog) replication

Full or incremental extraction using SQL is far simpler to implement, but also less scalable for large datasets with frequent changes. There are also trade-offs between full and incremental extractions that I discuss in the following section.

Binary Log replication, though more complex to implement, is better suited to cases where the data volume of changes in source tables is high, or there is a need for more frequent data ingestions from the MySQL source.

NOTE

Binlog replication is also a path to creating a *streaming data ingestion*. See the "Batch Versus Stream Ingestion" section of this chapter for more on the distinction between the two approaches as well as implementation patterns.

This section is relevant to those readers who have a MySQL data source they need to extract data from. However, if you'd like to set up a simple database so you can try the code samples, you have two options. First, you can install MySQL on your local machine or virtual machine for free. You can find an installer for your OS on the MySQL downloads page (*https://oreil.ly/p2-L1*).

Alternatively, you can create a fully managed Amazon RDS for MySQL instance in AWS (*https://oreil.ly/XahtN*). I find this method more straightforward, and it's nice not to create unnecessary clutter on my local machine!

WARNING

When you follow the linked instructions (*https://oreil.ly/CiVgC*) to set up an MySQL RDS database instance, you'll be prompted to set your database as publicly accessible. That's just fine for learning and working with sample data. In fact, it makes it much easier to connect from whatever machine you're running the samples in this section. However, for more robust security in a production setting, I suggest following the Amazon RDS security best practices (*https://oreil.ly/8DYsz*).

Note that just like the S3 pricing noted earlier, if you are no longer eligible for the free tier of AWS, there is a cost associated with doing so. Otherwise, it's free to set up and run! Just remember to delete your RDS instance when you're done so you don't forget and incur charges when your free tier expires.

The code samples in this section are quite simple and refer to a table named Orders in a MySQL database. Once you have a MySQL instance to work with, you can create the table and insert some sample rows by running the following SQL commands:

```
CREATE TABLE Orders (
  OrderId int,
  OrderStatus varchar(30),
  LastUpdated timestamp
);

INSERT INTO Orders
  VALUES(1,'Backordered', '2020-06-01 12:00:00');
INSERT INTO Orders
  VALUES(1,'Shipped', '2020-06-09 12:00:25');
INSERT INTO Orders
  VALUES(2,'Shipped', '2020-07-11 3:05:00');
INSERT INTO Orders
  VALUES(1,'Shipped', '2020-06-09 11:50:00');
INSERT INTO Orders
  VALUES(3,'Shipped', '2020-07-12 12:00:00');
```

Full or Incremental MySQL Table Extraction

When you need to ingest either all or a subset of columns from a MySQL table into a data warehouse or data lake, you can do so using either full extraction or incremental extraction.

In a *full extraction*, every record in the table is extracted on each run of the extraction job. This is the least complex approach, but for high-volume tables it can take a long time to run. For example, if you want to run a full extraction on a table called Orders, the SQL executed on the source MySQL database will look like this:

```
SELECT *
FROM Orders;
```

In an *incremental extraction*, only records from the source table that have changed or been added since the last run of the job are extracted. The timestamp of the last extraction can either be stored in an extraction job log table in the data warehouse or retrieved by querying the maximum timestamp in a `LastUpdated` column in the destination table in the warehouse. Using the fictional `Orders` table as an example, the SQL query executed on the source MySQL database will look like this:

```
SELECT *
FROM Orders
WHERE LastUpdated > {{ last_extraction_run} };
```

NOTE

For tables containing *immutable data* (meaning records can be inserted, but not updated), you can make use of the timestamp for when the record was created instead of a `LastUpdated` column.

The {{ `last_extraction_run` }} variable is a timestamp representing the most recent run of the extraction job. Most commonly it's queried from the destination table in the data warehouse. In that case, the following SQL would be executed in the data warehouse, with the resulting value used for {{ `last_extraction_run` }}:

```
SELECT MAX(LastUpdated)
FROM warehouse.Orders;
```

> ## Caching Last Updated Dates
>
> If the `Orders` table is quite large, you may store the value of the
> last updated record in a log table that can be quickly queried by
> the next run of the extraction job. Be sure to store the `MAX(Las
> tUpdated)` value from the destination table in the data ware-
> house and not the time the extraction job started or finished.
> Even a small lag in the time logged for job execution could
> mean missed or duplicated records from the source table in the
> next run.

Though incremental extraction is ideal for optimal performance, there are some downsides and reasons why it may not
be possible for a given table.

First, with this method deleted, rows are not captured. If a row
is deleted from the source MySQL table, you won't know, and it
will remain in the destination table as if nothing changed.

Second, the source table must have a reliable timestamp for
when it was last updated (the `LastUpdated` column in the previous example). It's not uncommon for source system tables to be
missing such a column or have one that is not updated reliably.
There's nothing stopping developers from updating records in
the source table and forgetting to update the `LastUpdated`
timestamp.

However, incremental extraction does make it easier to capture
updated rows. In the upcoming code samples, if a particular
row in the `Orders` table is updated, both the full and incremental extractions will bring back the latest version of the row. In
the full extract, that's true for all rows in the table as the extraction retrieves a full copy of the table. In the incremental extraction, only rows that have changed are retrieved.

When it comes time for the load step, full extracts are usually
loaded by first truncating the destination table and loading in
the newly extracted data. In that case, you're left with only the
latest version of the row in the data warehouse.

When loading data from an incremental extraction, the resulting data is appended to the data in the destination table. In that case, you have both the original record as well as the updated version. Having both can be valuable when it comes time to transform and analyze data, as I discuss in Chapter 6.

For example, Table 4-1 shows the original record for OrderId 1 in the MySQL database. When the order was placed by the customer, it was on back order. Table 4-2 shows the updated record in the MySQL database. As you can see, the order was updated because it shipped on 2020-06-09.

Table 4-1. Original state of OrderId 1

OrderId	OrderStatus	LastUpdated
1	Backordered	2020-06-01 12:00:00

Table 4-2. Updated state of OrderId 1

OrderId	OrderStatus	LastUpdated
1	Shipped	2020-06-09 12:00:25

When a full extraction is run, the destination table in the data warehouse is first truncated and then loaded with the output of the extraction. The result for OrderId 1 is the single record shown in Table 4-2. In an incremental extraction, however, the output of the extract is simply appended to the destination table in the data warehouse. The result is both the original and updated records for OrderId 1 being in the data warehouse, as illustrated in Table 4-3.

Table 4-3. All versions of OrderId 1 in the data warehouse

OrderId	OrderStatus	LastUpdated
1	Backordered	2020-06-01 12:00:00
1	Shipped	2020-06-09 12:00:25

You can learn more about loading full and incremental extractions in sections of Chapter 5 including "Loading Data into a Redshift Warehouse" on page 86.

WARNING

Never assume a `LastUpdated` column in a source system is reliably updated. Check with the owner of the source system and confirm before relying on it for an incremental extraction.

Both full and incremental extractions from a MySQL database can be implemented using SQL queries executed on the database but triggered by Python scripts. In addition to the Python libraries installed in previous sections, you'll need to install the PyMySQL library using `pip`:

```
(env) $ pip install pymysql
```

You'll also need to add a new section to the *pipeline.conf* file to store the connection information for the MySQL database:

```
[mysql_config]
hostname = my_host.com
port = 3306
username = my_user_name
password = my_password
database = db_name
```

Now create a new Python script named *extract_mysql_full.py*. You'll need to import several libraries, such as `pymysql`, which connects to the MySQL database, and the `csv` library so that you can structure and write out the extracted data in a flat file that's easy to import into a data warehouse in the load step of ingestion. Also, import `boto3` so that you can upload the resulting CSV file to your S3 bucket for later loading into the data warehouse:

```
import pymysql
import csv
import boto3
import configparser
```

Now you can initialize a connection to the MySQL database:

```
parser = configparser.ConfigParser()
parser.read("pipeline.conf")
hostname = parser.get("mysql_config", "hostname")
port = parser.get("mysql_config", "port")
username = parser.get("mysql_config", "username")
dbname = parser.get("mysql_config", "database")
password = parser.get("mysql_config", "password")

conn = pymysql.connect(host=hostname,
        user=username,
        password=password,
        db=dbname,
        port=int(port))

if conn is None:
  print("Error connecting to the MySQL database")
else:
  print("MySQL connection established!")
```

Run a full extraction of the Orders table from the earlier example. The following code will extract the entire contents of the table and write it to a pipe-delimited CSV file. To perform the extraction, it uses a cursor object from the pymysql library to execute the SELECT query:

```
m_query = "SELECT * FROM Orders;"
local_filename = "order_extract.csv"

m_cursor = conn.cursor()
m_cursor.execute(m_query)
results = m_cursor.fetchall()

with open(local_filename, 'w') as fp:
  csv_w = csv.writer(fp, delimiter='|')
  csv_w.writerows(results)
```

```
fp.close()
m_cursor.close()
conn.close()
```

Now that the CSV file is written locally, it needs to be uploaded to the S3 bucket for later loading into the data warehouse or other destination. Recall from "Setting Up Cloud File Storage" on page 37 that you set up an IAM user for the Boto3 library to use for authentication to the S3 bucket. You also stored the credentials in the aws_boto_credentials section of the *pipeline.conf* file. Here is the code to upload the CSV file to your S3 bucket:

```
# load the aws_boto_credentials values
parser = configparser.ConfigParser()
parser.read("pipeline.conf")
access_key = parser.get("aws_boto_credentials",
"access_key")
secret_key = parser.get("aws_boto_credentials",
"secret_key")
bucket_name = parser.get("aws_boto_credentials",
"bucket_name")

s3 = boto3.client('s3',
aws_access_key_id=access_key,
aws_secret_access_key=secret_key)

s3_file = local_filename

s3.upload_file(local_filename, bucket_name,
s3_file)
```

You can execute the script as follows:

```
(env) $ python extract_mysql_full.py
```

When the script is executed, the entire contents of the Orders table is now contained in a CSV file sitting in the S3 bucket waiting to be loaded into the data warehouse or other data store. See Chapter 5 for more on loading into the data store of your choice.

If you want to extract data incrementally, you'll need to make a few changes to the script. I suggest creating a copy of *extract_mysql_full.py* named *extract_mysql_incremental.py* as a starting point.

First, find the timestamp of the last record that was extracted from the source Orders table. To do that, query the MAX(LastUp dated) value from the Orders table in the data warehouse. In this example, I'll use a Redshift data warehouse (see "Configuring an Amazon Redshift Warehouse as a Destination" on page 83), but you can use the same logic with the warehouse of your choice.

To interact with your Redshift cluster, install the psycopg2 library, if you haven't already.

```
(env) $ pip install psycopg2
```

Here is the code to connect to and query the Redshift cluster to get the MAX(LastUpdated) value from the Orders table:

```
import psycopg2

# get db Redshift connection info
parser = configparser.ConfigParser()
parser.read("pipeline.conf")
dbname = parser.get("aws_creds", "database")
user = parser.get("aws_creds", "username")
password = parser.get("aws_creds", "password")
host = parser.get("aws_creds", "host")
port = parser.get("aws_creds", "port")

# connect to the redshift cluster
rs_conn = psycopg2.connect(
    "dbname=" + dbname
    + " user=" + user
    + " password=" + password
    + " host=" + host
    + " port=" + port)

rs_sql = """SELECT COALESCE(MAX(LastUpdated),
        '1900-01-01')
```

```
        FROM Orders;"""
rs_cursor = rs_conn.cursor()
rs_cursor.execute(rs_sql)
result = rs_cursor.fetchone()

# there's only one row and column returned
last_updated_warehouse = result[0]

rs_cursor.close()
rs_conn.commit()
```

Using the value stored in last_updated_warehouse, modify the extraction query run on the MySQL database to pull only those records from the Orders table that have been updated since the prior run of the extraction job. The new query contains a placeholder, represented by %s for the last_updated_warehouse value. The value is then passed into the cursor's .execute() function as a tuple (a data type used to store collections of data). This is the proper and secure way to add parameters to a SQL query to avoid possible SQL injection. Here is the updated code block for running the SQL query on the MySQL database:

```
m_query = """SELECT *
    FROM Orders
    WHERE LastUpdated > %s;"""
local_filename = "order_extract.csv"

m_cursor = conn.cursor()
m_cursor.execute(m_query, (last_updated_ware
house,))
```

The entire *extract_mysql_incremental.py* script for the incremental extraction (using a Redshift cluster for the last_updated value) looks like this:

```
import pymysql
import csv
import boto3
import configparser
import psycopg2
```

```python
# get db Redshift connection info
parser = configparser.ConfigParser()
parser.read("pipeline.conf")
dbname = parser.get("aws_creds", "database")
user = parser.get("aws_creds", "username")
password = parser.get("aws_creds", "password")
host = parser.get("aws_creds", "host")
port = parser.get("aws_creds", "port")

# connect to the redshift cluster
rs_conn = psycopg2.connect(
    "dbname=" + dbname
    + " user=" + user
    + " password=" + password
    + " host=" + host
    + " port=" + port)

rs_sql = """SELECT COALESCE(MAX(LastUpdated),
        '1900-01-01')
        FROM Orders;"""
rs_cursor = rs_conn.cursor()
rs_cursor.execute(rs_sql)
result = rs_cursor.fetchone()

# there's only one row and column returned
last_updated_warehouse = result[0]

rs_cursor.close()
rs_conn.commit()

# get the MySQL connection info and connect
parser = configparser.ConfigParser()
parser.read("pipeline.conf")
hostname = parser.get("mysql_config", "hostname")
port = parser.get("mysql_config", "port")
username = parser.get("mysql_config", "username")
dbname = parser.get("mysql_config", "database")
password = parser.get("mysql_config", "password")

conn = pymysql.connect(host=hostname,
```

```
            user=username,
            password=password,
            db=dbname,
            port=int(port))

if conn is None:
  print("Error connecting to the MySQL database")
else:
  print("MySQL connection established!")

m_query = """SELECT *
       FROM Orders
       WHERE LastUpdated > %s;"""
local_filename = "order_extract.csv"

m_cursor = conn.cursor()
m_cursor.execute(m_query, (last_updated_ware
house,))
results = m_cursor.fetchall()

with open(local_filename, 'w') as fp:
  csv_w = csv.writer(fp, delimiter='|')
  csv_w.writerows(results)

fp.close()
m_cursor.close()
conn.close()

# load the aws_boto_credentials values
parser = configparser.ConfigParser()
parser.read("pipeline.conf")
access_key = parser.get(
    "aws_boto_credentials",
    "access_key")
secret_key = parser.get(
    "aws_boto_credentials",
    "secret_key")
bucket_name = parser.get(
    "aws_boto_credentials",
    "bucket_name")
```

```
s3 = boto3.client(
    's3',
    aws_access_key_id=access_key,
    aws_secret_access_key=secret_key)

s3_file = local_filename

s3.upload_file(
    local_filename,
    bucket_name,
    s3_file)
```

WARNING

Beware of large extraction jobs—whether full or incremental—putting strain on the source MySQL database, and even blocking production queries from executing. Consult with the owner of the database and consider setting up a replica to extract from, rather than extracting from the primary source database.

Binary Log Replication of MySQL Data

Though more complex to implement, ingesting data from a MySQL database using the contents of the MySQL binlog to replicate changes is efficient in cases of high-volume ingestion needs.

NOTE

Binlog replication is a form of change data capture (CDC). Many source data stores have some form of CDC that you can use.

The MySQL binlog is a log that keeps a record of every operation performed in the database. For example, depending on how it's configured, it will log the specifics of every table creation or modification, as well as every INSERT, UPDATE, and DELETE operation. Though originally intended to replicate data to other MySQL instances, it's not hard to see why the contents of the binlog are so appealing to data engineers who want to ingest data into a data warehouse.

Consider Using a Prebuilt Framework

Due to the complexity of binlog replication, I highly suggest considering an open source framework or commercial product if you want to ingest data in this way. I discuss one such option in "Streaming Data Ingestions with Kafka and Debezium" on page 79. Some of commercial tools noted later in this chapter support binlog ingestion as well.

Because your data warehouse is likely not a MySQL database, it's not possible to simply use the built-in MySQL replication features. To make use of the binlog for data ingestion to a non-MySQL source, there are a number of steps to take:

1. Enable and configure the binlog on the MySQL server.

2. Run an initial full table extraction and load.

3. Extract from the binlog on a continuous basis.

4. Translate and load binlog extracts into the data warehouse.

Step 3 is not discussed in detail, but to use the binlog for ingestion, you must first populate the tables in the data warehouse with the current state of the MySQL database and then use the binlog to ingest subsequent changes. Doing so often involves putting a LOCK on the tables you want to extract, running a mysqldump of those tables, and then loading the result of the mysqldump into the warehouse before turning on the binlog ingestion.

Though it's best to refer to the latest MySQL binlog documentation (*https://oreil.ly/2Vdyf*) for instructions in enabling and configuring binary logging, I will walk through the key configuration values.

Consult with Source System Owners

Access to modify the configuration of binlogs on a MySQL source system is often reserved to system administrators. Data engineers who want to ingest the data should always work with the database owner before attempting to change binlog configuration as changes may impact other systems as well as the MySQL server itself.

There are two key settings to ensure on the MySQL database in regard to binlog configuration.

First, ensure that binary logging is enabled. Typically it is enabled by default, but you can check by running the following SQL query on the database (exact syntax may vary by MySQL distribution):

```
SELECT variable_value as bin_log_status
FROM performance_schema.global_variables
WHERE variable_name='log_bin';
```

If the binary logging is enabled, you'll see the following. If the status returned is `OFF`, then you'll need to consult the MySQL documentation for the relevant version to enable it.

```
+ - - - - - - - - - - - - - - - - -+
| bin_log_status :: |
+ - - - - - - - - - - - - - - - - -+
| ON |
+ - - - - - - - - - - - - - - - - -+
1 row in set (0.00 sec)
```

Next, ensure that the binary logging format is set appropriately. There are three formats supported in the recent version of MySQL:

- STATEMENT
- ROW
- MIXED

The STATEMENT format logs every SQL statement that inserts or modifies a row in the binlog. If you wanted to replicate data from one MySQL database to another, this format is useful. To replicate the data, you could just run all statements to reproduce the state of the database. However, because the extracted data is likely bound for a data warehouse running on a different platform, the SQL statements produced in the MySQL database may not be compatible with your data warehouse.

With the ROW format, every change to a row in a table is represented on a line of the binlog not as a SQL statement but rather the data in the row itself. This is the preferred format to use.

The MIXED format logs both STATEMENT- and ROW-formatted records in the binlog. Though it's possible to sift out just the ROW data later, unless the binlog is being used for another purpose, it's not necessary to enable MIXED, given the additional disk space that it takes up.

You can verify the current binlog format by running the following SQL query:

```
SELECT variable_value as bin_log_format
FROM performance_schema.global_variables
WHERE variable_name='binlog_format';
```

The statement will return the format that's currently active:

```
+ - - - - - - - - - - - - - - - - - - - - -+
| bin_log_format :: |
+ - - - - - - - - - - - - - - - - - - - - -+
| ROW |
+ - - - - - - - - - - - - - - - - - - - - -+
1 row in set (0.00 sec)
```

The binlog format as well as other configuration settings are typically set in the *my.cnf* file specific to the MySQL database instance. If you open the file, you'll see a row like the following included:

```
[mysqld]
binlog_format=row
........
```

Again, it's best to consult with the owner of the MySQL database or the latest MySQL documentation before modifying any configurations.

Now that binary logging is enabled in a ROW format, you can build a process to extract the relevant information from it and store it in a file to be loaded into your data warehouse.

There are three different types of ROW-formatted events that you'll want to pull from the binlog. For the sake of this ingestion example, you can ignore other events you find in the log, but in more advanced replication strategies, extracting events that modify the structure of a table is also of value. The events that you'll work with are as follows:

- WRITE_ROWS_EVENT
- UPDATE_ROWS_EVENT
- DELETE_ROWS_EVENT

Next, it's time to get the events from the binlog. Thankfully, there are some open source Python libraries available to get you started. One of the most popular is the python-mysql-replication project, which can be found on GitHub (*https://oreil.ly/QqBSu*). To get started, install it using pip:

```
(env) $ pip install mysql-replication
```

To get an idea of what the output from the binlog looks like, you can connect to the database and read from the binlog. In this example, I'll use the MySQL connection information added to the *pipeline.conf* file for the full and incremental ingestion example earlier in this section.

NOTE

The following example reads from the MySQL server's default binlog file. The default binlog filename and path are set in the log_bin variable, which is stored in the *my.cnf* file for the MySQL database. In some cases, binlogs are rotated over time (perhaps daily or hourly). If so, you will need to determine the file path based on the method of log rotation and file naming scheme chosen by the MySQL administrator and pass it as a value to the log_file parameter when creating the BinLogStreamReader instance. See the documentation for the BinLogStream Reader class (*https://oreil.ly/uzn0B*) for more.

```
from pymysqlreplication import BinLogStreamReader
from pymysqlreplication import row_event
import configparser
import pymysqlreplication

# get the MySQL connection info
parser = configparser.ConfigParser()
parser.read("pipeline.conf")
hostname = parser.get("mysql_config", "hostname")
port = parser.get("mysql_config", "port")
```

```
username = parser.get("mysql_config", "username")
password = parser.get("mysql_config", "password")

mysql_settings = {
    "host": hostname,
    "port": int(port),
    "user": username,
    "passwd": password
}

b_stream = BinLogStreamReader(
            connection_settings = mysql_settings,
            server_id=100,
            only_events=[row_event.DeleteRowsEvent,
                        row_event.WriteRowsEvent,
                        row_event.UpdateRowsEvent]
            )

for event in b_stream:
    event.dump()

b_stream.close()
```

There are a few things to note about the BinLogStreamReader object that's instantiated in the code sample. First, it connects to the MySQL database specified in the *pipeline.conf* file and reads from a specific binlog file. Next, the combination of the resume_stream=True setting and the log_pos value tells it to start reading the binlog at a specified point. In this case, that's position 1400. Finally, I tell BinLogStreamReader to only read the DeleteRowsEvent, WriteRowsEvent, and UpdateRowsEvent, events using the only_events parameter.

Next, the script iterates through all of the events and prints them in a human-readable format. For your database with the Orders table in it, you'll see something like this as output:

```
=== WriteRowsEvent ===
Date: 2020-06-01 12:00:00
Log position: 1400
Event size: 30
Read bytes: 20
Table: orders
Affected columns: 3
Changed rows: 1
Values:
--
* OrderId : 1
* OrderStatus : Backordered
* LastUpdated : 2020-06-01 12:00:00

=== UpdateRowsEvent ===
Date: 2020-06-09 12:00:25
Log position: 1401
Event size: 56
Read bytes: 15
Table: orders
Affected columns: 3
Changed rows: 1
Affected columns: 3
Values:
--
* OrderId : 1 => 1
* OrderStatus : Backordered => Shipped
* LastUpdated : 2020-06-01 12:00:00 => 2020-06-09
12:00:25
```

As you can see, there are two events that represent the INSERT
and UPDATE of OrderId 1, which was shown in Table 4-3. In this
fictional example, the two sequential binlog events are days
apart, but in reality there would be numerous events between
them, representing all changes made in the database.

The value of log_pos, which tells BinLogStreamReader where to start, is a value that you'll need to store somewhere in a table of your own to keep track of where to pick up when the next extract runs. I find it best to store the value in a log table in the data warehouse from which it can be read when the extraction starts and to which it can be written, with the position value of the final event when it finishes.

Though the code sample shows what the events look like in a human-readable format, to make the output easy to load into the data warehouse, it's necessary to do a couple more things:

- Parse and write the data in a different format. To simplify loading, the next code sample will write each event to a row in a CSV file.

- Write one file per table that you want to extract and load. Though the example binlog only contains events related to the Orders table, it's highly likely that in a real binlog, events related to other tables are included as well.

To address the first change, instead of using the .dump() function I will instead parse out the event attributes and write them to a CSV file. For the second, instead of writing a file for each table, for simplicity I will only write events related to the Orders table to a file called *orders_extract.csv*. In a fully implemented extraction, modify this code sample to group events by table and write multiple files, one for each table you want to ingest changes for. The last step in the final code sample uploads the CSV file to the S3 bucket so it can be loaded into the data warehouse, as described in detail in Chapter 5:

```
from pymysqlreplication import BinLogStreamReader
from pymysqlreplication import row_event
import configparser
```

```python
import pymysqlreplication
import csv
import boto3

# get the MySQL connection info
parser = configparser.ConfigParser()
parser.read("pipeline.conf")
hostname = parser.get("mysql_config", "hostname")
port = parser.get("mysql_config", "port")
username = parser.get("mysql_config", "username")
password = parser.get("mysql_config", "password")

mysql_settings = {
    "host": hostname,
    "port": int(port),
    "user": username,
    "passwd": password
}

b_stream = BinLogStreamReader(
            connection_settings = mysql_settings,
            server_id=100,
            only_events=[row_event.DeleteRowsEvent,
                        row_event.WriteRowsEvent,
                        row_event.UpdateRowsEvent]
            )

order_events = []

for binlogevent in b_stream:
  for row in binlogevent.rows:
    if binlogevent.table == 'orders':
      event = {}
      if isinstance(
            binlogevent,row_event.DeleteRowsEvent
        ):
        event["action"] = "delete"
        event.update(row["values"].items())
      elif isinstance(
            binlogevent,row_event.UpdateRowsEvent
```

```python
        ):
        event["action"] = "update"
        event.update(row["after_values"].items())
    elif isinstance(
            binlogevent,row_event.WriteRowsEvent
        ):
        event["action"] = "insert"
        event.update(row["values"].items())

    order_events.append(event)

b_stream.close()

keys = order_events[0].keys()
local_filename = 'orders_extract.csv'
with open(
        local_filename,
        'w',
        newline='') as output_file:
    dict_writer = csv.DictWriter(
                output_file, keys,delimiter='|')
    dict_writer.writerows(order_events)

# load the aws_boto_credentials values
parser = configparser.ConfigParser()
parser.read("pipeline.conf")
access_key = parser.get(
                "aws_boto_credentials",
                "access_key")
secret_key = parser.get(
                "aws_boto_credentials",
                "secret_key")
bucket_name = parser.get(
                "aws_boto_credentials",
                "bucket_name")

s3 = boto3.client(
    's3',
    aws_access_key_id=access_key,
    aws_secret_access_key=secret_key)
```

```
s3_file = local_filename

s3.upload_file(
    local_filename,
    bucket_name,
    s3_file)
```

After execution, *orders_extract.csv* will look like this:

```
insert|1|Backordered|2020-06-01 12:00:00
update|1|Shipped|2020-06-09 12:00:25
```

As I discuss in Chapter 5, the format of the resulting CSV file is optimized for fast loading. Making sense of the data that's been extracted is a job for the transform step in a pipeline, reviewed in detail in Chapter 6.

Extracting Data from a PostgreSQL Database

Just like MySQL, ingesting data from a PostgreSQL (commonly known as Postgres) database can be done in one of two ways: either with full or incremental extractions using SQL or by leveraging features of the database meant to support replication to other nodes. In the case of Postgres, there are a few ways to do this, but this chapter will focus on one method: turning the Postgres *write-ahead log* (WAL) into a data stream.

Like the previous section, this one is intended for those who need to ingest data from an existing Postgres database. However, if you'd like to just try the code samples, you can set up Postgres either by installing on your local machine (*https://oreil.ly/3KId7*), or in AWS by using an a RDS instance (*https://oreil.ly/SWj3g*), which I recommend. See the previous section for notes on pricing and security-related best practices for RDS MySQL, as they apply to RDS Postgres as well.

The code samples in this section are quite simple and refer to a table named Orders in a Postgres database. Once you have a Postgres instance to work with, you can create the table and insert some sample rows by running the following SQL commands:

```
CREATE TABLE Orders (
  OrderId int,
  OrderStatus varchar(30),
  LastUpdated timestamp
);

INSERT INTO Orders
  VALUES(1,'Backordered', '2020-06-01 12:00:00');
INSERT INTO Orders
  VALUES(1,'Shipped', '2020-06-09 12:00:25');
INSERT INTO Orders
  VALUES(2,'Shipped', '2020-07-11 3:05:00');
INSERT INTO Orders
  VALUES(1,'Shipped', '2020-06-09 11:50:00');
INSERT INTO Orders
  VALUES(3,'Shipped', '2020-07-12 12:00:00');
```

Full or Incremental Postgres Table Extraction

This method is similar to full and incremental and full extractions demonstrated in "Extracting Data from a MySQL Database" on page 39. It's so similar that I won't go into detail here beyond one difference in the code. Like the example in that section, this one will extract data from a table called Orders in a source database, write it to a CSV file, and then upload it to an S3 bucket.

The only difference in this section is the Python library I'll use to extract the data. Instead of PyMySQL, I'll be using pyscopg2 to connect to a Postgres database. If you have not already installed it, you can do so using pip:

```
(env) $ pip install pyscopg2
```

You'll also need to add a new section to the *pipeline.conf* file with the connection information for the Postgres database:

```
[postgres_config]
host = myhost.com
```

```
port = 5432
username = my_username
password = my_password
database = db_name
```

The code to run the full extraction of the Orders table is nearly
identical to the sample from the MySQL section, but as you can
see, it uses pyscopg2 to connect to the source database and to
run the query. Here it is in its entirety:

```python
import psycopg2
import csv
import boto3
import configparser

parser = configparser.ConfigParser()
parser.read("pipeline.conf")
dbname = parser.get("postgres_config", "database")
user = parser.get("postgres_config", "username")
password = parser.get("postgres_config",
    "password")
host = parser.get("postgres_config", "host")
port = parser.get("postgres_config", "port")

conn = psycopg2.connect(
        "dbname=" + dbname
        + " user=" + user
        + " password=" + password
        + " host=" + host,
        port = port)

m_query = "SELECT * FROM Orders;"
local_filename = "order_extract.csv"

m_cursor = conn.cursor()
m_cursor.execute(m_query)
results = m_cursor.fetchall()

with open(local_filename, 'w') as fp:
  csv_w = csv.writer(fp, delimiter='|')
  csv_w.writerows(results)
```

```
        fp.close()
        m_cursor.close()
        conn.close()

        # load the aws_boto_credentials values
        parser = configparser.ConfigParser()
        parser.read("pipeline.conf")
        access_key = parser.get(
                        "aws_boto_credentials",
                        "access_key")
        secret_key = parser.get(
                        "aws_boto_credentials",
                        "secret_key")
        bucket_name = parser.get(
                        "aws_boto_credentials",
                        "bucket_name")

        s3 = boto3.client(
            's3',
            aws_access_key_id = access_key,
            aws_secret_access_key = secret_key)

        s3_file = local_filename

        s3.upload_file(
            local_filename,
            bucket_name,
            s3_file)
```

Modifying the incremental version shown in the MySQL section is just as simple. All you need to do is make use of psy
copg2 instead of PyMySQL.

Replicating Data Using the Write-Ahead Log

Like the MySQL binlog (as discussed in the previous section),
the Postgres WAL can be used as a method of CDC for extraction. Also like the MySQL binlog, using the WAL for data
ingestion in a pipeline is quite complex.

Though you can take a similar, simplified approach to the one used as an example with the MySQL binlog, I suggest using an open source distributed platform called Debezium to stream the contents of the Postgres WAL to an S3 bucket or data warehouse.

Though the specifics of configuring and running Debezium services are a topic worth dedicating an entire book to, I give an overview of Debezium and how it can be used for data ingestions in "Streaming Data Ingestions with Kafka and Debezium" on page 79. You can learn more about how it can be used for Postgres CDC there.

Extracting Data from MongoDB

This example illustrates how to extract a subset of MongoDB documents from a collection. In this sample MongoDB collection, documents represent events logged from some system such as a web server. Each document has a timestamp of when it was created, as well as a number of properties that the sample code extracts a subset of. After the extraction is complete, the data is written to a CSV file and stored in an S3 bucket so that it can be loaded into a data warehouse in a future step (see Chapter 5).

To connect to the MongoDB database, you'll need to first install the PyMongo library. As with other Python libraries, you can install it using `pip`:

```
(env) $ pip install pymongo
```

You can of course modify the following sample code to connect to your own MongoDB instance and extract data from your documents. However, if you'd like to run the sample as is, you can do so by creating a MongoDB cluster for free with MongoDB Atlas. Atlas is a fully managed MongoDB service and includes a free-for-life tier with plenty of storage and computing power for learning and running samples like the one I provide. You can upgrade to a paid plan for production deployments.

You can learn how to create a free MongoDB cluster in Atlas, create a database, and configure it so that you can connect via a Python script running on your local machine by following these instructions (*https://oreil.ly/DIPdo*).

You'll need to install one more Python library named dnspy thon to support pymongo in connecting to your cluster hosted in MongoDB Atlas. You can install it using pip:

```
(env) $ pip install dnspython
```

Next, add a new section to the *pipeline.conf* file with connection information for the MongoDB instance you'll be extracting data from. Fill in each line with your own connection details. If you're using MongoDB Atlas and can't recall these values from when you set up your cluster, you can learn how to find them by reading the Atlas docs (*https://oreil.ly/Zdynu*).

```
[mongo_config]
hostname = my_host.com
username = mongo_user
password = mongo_password
database = my_database
collection = my_collection
```

Before creating and running the extraction script, you can insert some sample data to work with. Create a file called *sample_mongodb.py* with the following code:

```
from pymongo import MongoClient
import datetime
import configparser

# load the mongo_config values
parser = configparser.ConfigParser()
parser.read("pipeline.conf")
hostname = parser.get("mongo_config", "hostname")
username = parser.get("mongo_config", "username")
password = parser.get("mongo_config", "password")
database_name = parser.get("mongo_config",
                          "database")
collection_name = parser.get("mongo_config",
```

```python
                       "collection")

mongo_client = MongoClient(
                "mongodb+srv://" + username
                + ":" + password
                + "@" + hostname
                + "/" + database_name
                + "?retryWrites=true&"
                + "w=majority&ssl=true&"
                + "ssl_cert_reqs=CERT_NONE")

# connect to the db where the collection resides
mongo_db = mongo_client[database_name]

# choose the collection to query documents from
mongo_collection = mongo_db[collection_name]

event_1 = {
  "event_id": 1,
  "event_timestamp": datetime.datetime.today(),
  "event_name": "signup"
}

event_2 = {
  "event_id": 2,
  "event_timestamp": datetime.datetime.today(),
  "event_name": "pageview"
}

event_3 = {
  "event_id": 3,
  "event_timestamp": datetime.datetime.today(),
  "event_name": "login"
}

# insert the 3 documents
mongo_collection.insert_one(event_1)
mongo_collection.insert_one(event_2)
mongo_collection.insert_one(event_3)
```

When you execute it, the three documents will be inserted into your MongoDB collection:

```
(env) $ python sample_mongodb.py
```

Now create a new Python script called *mongo_extract.py* so you can add the following code blocks to it.

First, import PyMongo and Boto3 so that you can extract data from the MongoDB database and store the results in an S3 bucket. Also import the csv library so that you can structure and write out the extracted data in a flat file that's easy to import into a data warehouse in the load step of ingestion. Finally, you'll need some datetime functions for this example so that you can iterate through the sample event data in the MongoDB collection:

```
from pymongo import MongoClient
import csv
import boto3
import datetime
from datetime import timedelta
import configparser
```

Next, connect to the MongoDB instance specified in the pipe lines.conf file, and create a collection object where the documents you want to extract are stored:

```
# load the mongo_config values
parser = configparser.ConfigParser()
parser.read("pipeline.conf")
hostname = parser.get("mongo_config", "hostname")
username = parser.get("mongo_config", "username")
password = parser.get("mongo_config", "password")
database_name = parser.get("mongo_config",
                    "database")
collection_name = parser.get("mongo_config",
                    "collection")

mongo_client = MongoClient(
                    "mongodb+srv://" + username
                    + ":" + password
```

```
                      + "@" + hostname
                      + "/" + database_name
                      + "?retryWrites=true&"
                      + "w=majority&ssl=true&"
                      + "ssl_cert_reqs=CERT_NONE")

  # connect to the db where the collection resides
  mongo_db = mongo_client[database_name]

  # choose the collection to query documents from
  mongo_collection = mongo_db[collection_name]
```

Now it's time to query the documents to extract. You can do this by calling the .find() function on mongo_collection to query the documents you're looking for. In the following example, you'll grab all documents with a event_timestamp field value between two dates defined in the script.

NOTE

Extracting immutable data such as log records or generic "event" records from a data store by date range is a common use case. Although the sample code uses a datetime range defined in the script, it's more likely you'll pass in a datetime range to the script, or have the script query your data warehouse to get the datetime of the last event loaded, and extract subsequent records from the source data store. See "Extracting Data from a MySQL Database" on page 39 for an example of doing so.

```
start_date = datetime.datetime.today() + time
delta(days = -1)
end_date = start_date + timedelta(days = 1 )

mongo_query = { "$and":[{"event_timestamp" :
{ "$gte": start_date }}, {"event_timestamp" :
{ "$lt": end_date }}] }
```

```
event_docs = mongo_collection.find(mongo_query,
batch_size=3000)
```

NOTE

The batch_size parameter in this example is set to 3000. PyMongo makes a round-trip to the MongoDB host for each batch. For example, if the result_docs Cursor has 6,000 results, it will take two trips to the MongoDB host to pull all the documents down to the machine where your Python script is running. What you set as the batch size value is up to you and will depend on the trade-off of storing more documents in memory on the system running the extract versus making lots of round trips to the MongoDB instance.

The result of the preceding code is a Cursor named event_docs that I'll use to iterate through the resulting documents. Recall that in this simplified example, each document represents an event that was generated from a system such as a web server. An event might represent something like a user logging in, viewing a page, or submitting a feedback form. Though the documents might have dozens of fields to represent things like the browser the user logged in with, I take just a few fields for this example:

```
# create a blank list to store the results
all_events = []

# iterate through the cursor
for doc in event_docs:
    # Include default values
    event_id = str(doc.get("event_id", -1))
    event_timestamp = doc.get(
                        "event_timestamp", None)
    event_name = doc.get("event_name", None)

    # add all the event properties into a list
```

```
current_event = []
current_event.append(event_id)
current_event.append(event_timestamp)
current_event.append(event_name)

# add the event to the final list of events
all_events.append(current_event)
```

I'm including a default value in the doc.get() function call (–1 or None). Why? The nature of unstructured document data means that it's possible for fields to go missing from a document altogether. In other words, you can't assume that each of the documents you're iterating through has an "event_name" or any other field. In those cases, tell doc.get() to return a None value instead of throwing an error.

After iterating through all the events in event_docs, the all_events list is ready to be written to a CSV file. To do so, you'll make use of the csv module, which is included in the standard Python distribution and was imported earlier in this example:

```
export_file = "export_file.csv"

with open(export_file, 'w') as fp:
        csvw = csv.writer(fp, delimiter='|')
        csvw.writerows(all_events)

fp.close()
```

Now, upload the CSV file to the S3 bucket that you configured in "Setting Up Cloud File Storage" on page 37. To do so, use the Boto3 library:

```
# load the aws_boto_credentials values
parser = configparser.ConfigParser()
parser.read("pipeline.conf")
access_key = parser.get("aws_boto_credentials",
                "access_key")
secret_key = parser.get("aws_boto_credentials",
                "secret_key")
```

```
bucket_name = parser.get("aws_boto_credentials",
                         "bucket_name")

s3 = boto3.client('s3',
        aws_access_key_id=access_key,
        aws_secret_access_key=secret_key)

s3_file = export_file

s3.upload_file(export_file, bucket_name, s3_file)
```

That's it! The data you extracted from the MongoDB collection
is now sitting in the S3 bucket waiting to be loaded into the
data warehouse or other data store. If you used the sample data
provided, the contents of *export_file.csv* will look something
like this:

```
1|2020-12-13 11:01:37.942000|signup
2|2020-12-13 11:01:37.942000|pageview
3|2020-12-13 11:01:37.942000|login
```

See Chapter 5 for more on loading the data into the data store
of your choice.

Extracting Data from a REST API

REST APIs are a common source to extract data from. You may
need to ingest data from an API that your organization created
and maintains, or from an API from an external service or vendor that your organization uses, such as Salesforce, HubSpot,
or Twitter. No matter the API, there's a common pattern for
data extraction that I'll use in the simple example that follows:

1. Send an HTTP GET request to the API endpoint.

2. Accept the response, which is most likely formatted in
   JSON.

3. Parse the response and "flatten" it into a CSV file that you
   can later load into the data warehouse.

In this example, I'll connect to an API called Open Notify. The API has several endpoints, each returning data from NASA about things happening in space. I'll query the endpoint that returns the next five times that the International Space Station (ISS) will pass over the given location on Earth.

Python Libraries for Specific APIs

It's possible to query any REST API using the Python code sample in this section. However, you can save yourself some time and effort if there is a Python library built specifically for the API you'd like to query. For example, the tweepy library makes it easy for a Python developer to access the Twitter API and handle common Twitter data structures such as tweets and users.

Before I share the Python code for querying the endpoint, you can see what the output of a simple query looks like by typing the following URL into your browser:

```
http://api.open-notify.org/iss-pass.json?
lat=42.36&lon=71.05
```

The resulting JSON looks like this:

```
{
  "message": "success",
  "request": {
```

```
       "altitude": 100,
       "datetime": 1596384217,
       "latitude": 42.36,
       "longitude": 71.05,
       "passes": 5
     },
     "response": [
       {
         "duration": 623,
         "risetime": 1596384449
       },
       {
         "duration": 169,
         "risetime": 1596390428
       },
       {
         "duration": 482,
         "risetime": 1596438949
       },
       {
         "duration": 652,
         "risetime": 1596444637
       },
       {
         "duration": 624,
         "risetime": 1596450474
       }
     ]
   }
```

The goal of this extraction is to retrieve the data in the response and format it in a CSV file with one line for each time and duration of each pass that the ISS will make over the lat/long pair. For example, the first two lines of the CSV file will be as follows:

```
42.36,|71.05|623|1596384449
42.36,|71.05|169|1596390428
```

To query the API and handle the response in Python, you'll need to install the requests library. requests makes HTTP requests and responses easy to work with in Python. You can install it with pip:

```
(env) $ pip install requests
```

Now, you can use requests to query the API endpoint, get back the response, and print out the resulting JSON, which will look like what you saw in your browser:

```
import requests

lat = 42.36
lon = 71.05
lat_log_params = {"lat": lat, "lon": lon}

api_response = requests.get(
    "http://api.open-notify.org/iss-pass.json", par
ams=lat_log_params)

print(api_response.content)
```

Instead of printing out the JSON, I'll iterate through the response, parse out the values for duration and risetime, write the results to a CSV file, and upload the file to the S3 bucket.

To parse the JSON response, I'll import the Python json library. There's no need to install it as it comes with the standard Python installation. Next, I'll import the csv library, which is also included in the standard Python distribution for writing the CSV file. Finally, I'll use the configparser library to get the credentials required by the Boto3 library to upload the CSV file to the S3 bucket:

```
import requests
import json
import configparser
import csv
import boto3
```

Next, query the API just as you did before:

```
lat = 42.36
lon = 71.05
```

```
lat_log_params = {"lat": lat, "lon": lon}

api_response = requests.get(
    "http://api.open-notify.org/iss-pass.json", par
ams=lat_log_params)
```

Now, it's time to iterate through the response, store the results in a Python list called all_passes, and save the results to a CSV file. Note that I also store the lat and long from the request even though they are not included in the response. They are needed on each line of the CSV file so that the pass times are associated with the correct lat and long when loaded into the data warehouse:

```
# create a json object from the response content
response_json = json.loads(api_response.content)

all_passes = []
for response in response_json['response']:
    current_pass = []

    #store the lat/log from the request
    current_pass.append(lat)
    current_pass.append(lon)

    # store the duration and risetime of the pass
    current_pass.append(response['duration'])
    current_pass.append(response['risetime'])

    all_passes.append(current_pass)

export_file = "export_file.csv"

with open(export_file, 'w') as fp:
        csvw = csv.writer(fp, delimiter='|')
        csvw.writerows(all_passes)

fp.close()
```

Finally, upload the CSV file to the S3 bucket using the Boto3 library:

```
# load the aws_boto_credentials values
parser = configparser.ConfigParser()
parser.read("pipeline.conf")
access_key = parser.get("aws_boto_credentials",
                "access_key")
secret_key = parser.get("aws_boto_credentials",
                "secret_key")
bucket_name = parser.get("aws_boto_credentials",
                "bucket_name")

s3 = boto3.client(
    's3',
    aws_access_key_id=access_key,
    aws_secret_access_key=secret_key)

s3.upload_file(
    export_file,
    bucket_name,
    export_file)
```

Streaming Data Ingestions with Kafka and Debezium

When it comes to ingesting data from a CDC system such as MySQL binlogs or Postgres WALs, there's no simple solution without some help from a great framework.

Debezium is a distributed system made up of several open source services that capture row-level changes from common CDC systems and then streams them as events that are consumable by other systems. There are three primary components of a Debezium installation:

- *Apache Zookeeper* manages the distributed environment and handles configuration across each service.
- *Apache Kafka* is a distributed streaming platform that is commonly used to build highly scalable data pipelines.

- *Apache Kafka Connect* is a tool to connect Kafka with other systems so that the data can be easily streamed via Kafka. *Connectors* are built for systems like MySQL and Postgres and turn data from their CDC systems (binlogs and WAL) into *Kakfa topics*.

Kafka exchanges messages that are organized by *topic*. One system might publish to a topic, while one or more might consume, or subscribe to, the topic.

Debezium ties these systems together and includes connectors for common CDC implementations. For example, I discussed the challenges for CDC in "Extracting Data from a MySQL Database" on page 39 and "Extracting Data from a PostgreSQL Database" on page 63. Thankfully, there are connectors already built to "listen" to the MySQL binlog and Postgres WAL. The data is then routed through Kakfa as records in a topic and consumed into a destination such as an S3 bucket, Snowflake, or Redshift data warehouse using another connector. Figure 4-1 illustrates an example of using Debezium, and its individual components, to send the events created by a MySQL binlog into a Snowflake data warehouse.

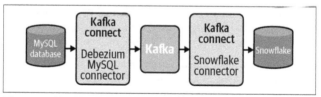

Figure 4-1. Using components of Debezium for CDC from MySQL to Snowflake.

As of this writing, there are a number of Debezium connectors already built for source systems that you may find yourself needing to ingest from:

- MongoDB
- MySQL

- PostgreSQL
- Microsoft SQL Server
- Oracle
- Db2
- Cassandra

There are also Kafka Connect connectors for the most common data warehouses and storage systems, such as S3 and Snowflake.

Though Debezium, and Kafka itself, is a subject that justifies its own book, I do want to point out its value if you decide that CDC is a method you want to use for data ingestion. The simple example I used in the MySQL extraction section of this chapter is functional; however, if you want to use CDC at scale, I highly suggest using something like Debezium rather than building an existing platform like Debezium on your own!

TIP

The Debezium documentation (*https://oreil.ly/9igMR*) is excellent and a great starting point for learning about the system.

Data Ingestion: Loading Data

In Chapter 4, you extracted data from your desired source system. Now it's time to complete the data ingestion by loading the data into your Redshift data warehouse. How you load depends on what the output of your data extraction looks like. In this section I will describe how to load data extracted into CSV files with the values corresponding to each column in a table, as well as extraction output containing CDC-formatted data.

Configuring an Amazon Redshift Warehouse as a Destination

If you're using Amazon Redshift for your data warehouse, integration with S3 for loading data after it has been extracted is quite simple. The first step is to create an IAM role for loading data if you don't already have one.

For instructions on setting up an Amazon Redshift cluster, check the latest documentation and pricing, including free trials (*https://oreil.ly/YSaxa*).

Don't Confuse IAM Roles and IAM Users

In "Setting Up Cloud File Storage" on page 37, you created an IAM user that has read and write access set on the S3 bucket that you'll use throughout this section. In this section you're creating an IAM *role*, which you'll assign permissions specific to reading from S3 directly to your Redshift cluster.

To create the role, follow these instructions or check the AWS documentation (*https://oreil.ly/QEJzH*) for the latest details:

1. Under the Services menu in the AWS console (or top navigation bar), navigate to IAM.

2. On the left navigation menu, select Roles, and then click the "Create role" button.

3. You'll be presented with a list of AWS services to select from. Find and select Redshift.

4. Under "Select your use case," choose Redshift – Customizable.

5. On the next page (Attach permission policies), search for and select AmazonS3ReadOnlyAccess, and click Next.

6. Give your role a name (for example, "RedshiftLoadRole") and click "Create role."

7. Click the name of the new role, and copy the *role Amazon resource name* (ARN) so you can use it in later in this chapter. You can find this later in the IAM console under

the role properties as well. The ARN looks like this:
`arn:aws:iam::<aws-account-id>:role/<role-name>`.

Now you can associate the IAM role you just created with your Redshift cluster. To do so, follow these steps or check the Redshift documentation (*https://oreil.ly/uHLEk*) for more details.

NOTE

Your cluster will take a minute or two to apply the changes, but it will still be accessible during this time.

---

1. Go back to the AWS Services menu and go to Amazon Redshift.

2. In the navigation menu, select Clusters and select the cluster you want to load data into.

3. Under Actions, click "Manage IAM roles."

4. On the "Manage IAM roles" page that loads, you will be able to select your role in the "Available roles" drop-down. Then click "Add IAM role."

5. Click Done.

Finally, add another section to the *pipeline.conf* file that you created in "Setting Up Cloud File Storage" on page 37 with your Redshift credentials and the name of the IAM role you just created. You can find your Redshift cluster connection information on the AWS Redshift Console page:

```
[aws_creds]
database = my_warehouse
username = pipeline_user
password = weifj4tji4j
host = my_example.4754875843.us-
east-1.redshift.amazonaws.com
```

```
port = 5439
iam_role = RedshiftLoadRole
```

Loading Data into a Redshift Warehouse

Loading data into Redshift that's been extracted and stored as
values corresponding to each column in a table in your S3
bucket as a CSV file is relatively straightforward. Data in this
format is most common and is the result of extracting data
from a source such as a MySQL or MongoDB database. Each
row in the CSV file to be loaded corresponds to a record to be
loaded into the destination Redshift table, and each column in
the CSV corresponds to the column in the destination table. If
you extracted events from a MySQL binlog or other CDC log,
see the following section for instructions on loading.

The most efficient way to load data from S3 into Redshift is to
use the COPY command. COPY can be executed as a SQL statement in whatever SQL client you use to query your Redshift
cluster or in a Python script using the Boto3 library. COPY
appends the data you're loading to the existing rows in the destination table.

The COPY command's syntax is as follows. All bracketed ([]) items are optional:

```
COPY table_name
[ column_list ]
FROM source_file
authorization
[ [ FORMAT ] [ AS ] data_format ]
[ parameter [ argument ] [, .. ] ]
```

NOTE

You can learn more about additional options, and the COPY command in general, in the AWS documentation (*https://oreil.ly/0uWo8*).

In its simplest form, using IAM role authorization as specified in Chapter 4 and a file in your S3 bucket looks something like this when run from a SQL client:

```
COPY my_schema.my_table
FROM 's3://bucket-name/file.csv'
iam_role '<my-arn>';
```

As you'll recall from "Configuring an Amazon Redshift Warehouse as a Destination" on page 83, the ARN is formatted like this:

```
arn:aws:iam::<aws-account-id>:role/<role-name>
```

If you named the role RedshiftLoadRole, then the COPY command syntax looks like the following. Note that the numeric value in the ARN is specific to your AWS account:

```
COPY my_schema.my_table
FROM 's3://bucket-name/file.csv'
iam_role 'arn:aws:iam::222:role/RedshiftLoadRole';
```

When executed, the contents of *file.csv* are appended to a table called my_table in the my_schema schema of your Redshift cluster.

By default, the COPY command inserts data into the columns of the destination table in the same order as the fields in the input file. In other words, unless you specify otherwise, the order of the fields in the CSV you're loading in this example should match the order of the columns in the destination table in Redshift. If you'd like to specify the column order, you can do so by adding the names of the destination columns in an order that matches your input file, as shown here:

```
COPY my_schema.my_table (column_1, column_2, ....)
FROM 's3://bucket-name/file.csv'
iam_role 'arn:aws:iam::222:role/RedshiftLoadRole';
```

It's also possible to use the Boto3 library to implement the COPY command in a Python script. In fact, following the template of the data extraction examples in Chapter 4, loading data via Python makes for a more standardized data pipeline.

To interact with the Redshift cluster you configured earlier in this chapter, you'll need to install the psycopg2 library:

```
(env) $ pip install psycopg2
```

Now you can start writing your Python script. Create a new file called *copy_to_redshift.py* and add the following three code blocks.

The first step is to import boto3 to interact with the S3 bucket, psycopg2 to run the COPY command on the Redshift cluster, and the configparser library to read the *pipeline.conf* file:

```
import boto3
import configparser
import psycopg2
```

Next, connect to the Redshift cluster using the `psycopg2.con` nect function and credentials stored in the *pipeline.conf* file:

```
parser = configparser.ConfigParser()
parser.read("pipeline.conf")
dbname = parser.get("aws_creds", "database")
user = parser.get("aws_creds", "username")
password = parser.get("aws_creds", "password")
host = parser.get("aws_creds", "host")
port = parser.get("aws_creds", "port")

# connect to the redshift cluster
rs_conn = psycopg2.connect(
    "dbname=" + dbname
    + " user=" + user
    + " password=" + password
    + " host=" + host
    + " port=" + port)
```

Now you can execute the COPY command using a psycopg2 Cur sor object. Run the same COPY command that you ran manually earlier in the section, but instead of hard-coding the AWS account ID and IAM role name, load those values from the *pipeline.conf* file:

```
# load the account_id and iam_role from the
# conf files
parser = configparser.ConfigParser()
parser.read("pipeline.conf")
account_id = parser.get("aws_boto_credentials",
                "account_id")
iam_role = parser.get("aws_creds", "iam_role")
bucket_name = parser.get("aws_boto_credentials",
                "bucket_name")

# run the COPY command to load the file into Red
shift
file_path = ("s3://"
```

```
    + bucket_name
    + "/order_extract.csv")
role_string = ("arn:aws:iam::"
    + account_id
    + ":role/" + iam_role)

sql = "COPY public.Orders"
sql = sql + " from %s "
sql = sql + " iam_role %s;"

# create a cursor object and execute the COPY
cur = rs_conn.cursor()
cur.execute(sql,(file_path, role_string))

# close the cursor and commit the transaction
cur.close()
rs_conn.commit()

# close the connection
rs_conn.close()
```

Before you can run the script, you'll need to create the destination table if it does not already exist. In this example, I'm loading data that was extracted into the *order_extract.csv* file in "Full or Incremental MySQL Table Extraction" on page 41. You can of course load whatever data you'd like. Just make sure the destination table has the structure to match. To create the destination table on your cluster, run the following SQL via the Redshift Query Editor or other application connected to your cluster:

```
CREATE TABLE public.Orders (
  OrderId int,
  OrderStatus varchar(30),
  LastUpdated timestamp
);
```

Finally, run the script as follows:

```
(env) $ python copy_to_redshift.py
```

Incremental Versus Full Loads

In the previous code sample, the COPY command loaded the data from the extracted CSV file directly into a table in the Redshift cluster. If the data in the CSV file came from an incremental extract of an immutable source (as is the case with something like immutable event data or other "insert-only" dataset), then there's nothing more to do. However, if the data in the CSV file contains updated records as well as inserts or the entire contents of the source table, then you have a bit more work to do, or at least considerations to take into account.

Take the case of the Orders table from "Full or Incremental MySQL Table Extraction" on page 41. That means the data you're loading from the CSV file was extracted either in full or incrementally from the source MySQL table.

If the data was extracted in full, then you have one small addition to make to the loading script. Truncate the destination table in Redshift (using TRUNCATE) before you run the COPY operation. The updated code snippet looks like this:

```python
import boto3
import configparser
import psycopg2

parser = configparser.ConfigParser()
parser.read("pipeline.conf")
dbname = parser.get("aws_creds", "database")
user = parser.get("aws_creds", "username")
password = parser.get("aws_creds", "password")
host = parser.get("aws_creds", "host")
port = parser.get("aws_creds", "port")

# connect to the redshift cluster
rs_conn = psycopg2.connect(
    "dbname=" + dbname
    + " user=" + user
    + " password=" + password
    + " host=" + host
    + " port=" + port)
```

```python
parser = configparser.ConfigParser()
parser.read("pipeline.conf")
account_id = parser.get("aws_boto_credentials",
                        "account_id")
iam_role = parser.get("aws_creds", "iam_role")
bucket_name = parser.get("aws_boto_credentials",
                         "bucket_name")

# truncate the destination table
sql = "TRUNCATE public.Orders;"
cur = rs_conn.cursor()
cur.execute(sql)

cur.close()
rs_conn.commit()

# run the COPY command to load the file into Red
shift
file_path = ("s3://"
    + bucket_name
    + "/order_extract.csv")
role_string = ("arn:aws:iam::"
    + account_id
    + ":role/" + iam_role)

sql = "COPY public.Orders"
sql = sql + " from %s "
sql = sql + " iam_role %s;"

# create a cursor object and execute the COPY com
mand
cur = rs_conn.cursor()
cur.execute(sql,(file_path, role_string))

# close the cursor and commit the transaction
cur.close()
rs_conn.commit()
```

```
# close the connection
rs_conn.close()
```

If the data was incrementally extracted, you don't want to truncate the destination table. If you did, all you'd have left are the updated records from the last run of the extraction job. There are a few ways you can handle data extracted in this way, but the best is to keep things simple.

In this case, you can simply load the data using the COPY command (no TRUNCATE!) and rely on the timestamp stating when the record was last updated to later identify which record is the latest or to look back at an historical record. For example, let's say that a record in the source table was modified and thus present in the CSV file being loaded. After loading, you'd see something like Table 5-1 in the Redshift destination table.

Table 5-1. The Orders table in Redshift

OrderId	OrderStatus	LastUpdated
1	Backordered	2020-06-01 17:00:00
1	Shipped	2020-06-09 12:00:25

As you can see in Table 5-1, the order with an ID value of 1 is in the table twice. The first record existed prior to the latest load, and the second was just loaded from the CSV file. The first record came in due to an update to the record on 2020-06-01, when the order was in a Backordered state. It was updated again on 2020-06-09, when it Shipped and included in the last CSV file you loaded.

From the standpoint of historical record keeping, it's ideal to have both of these records in the destination table. Later in the transform phase of the pipeline, an analyst can choose to use either or both of the records, depending on the needs of a particular analysis. Perhaps they want to know how long the order was in a backordered state. They need both records to do that. If they want to know the current status of the order, they have that as well.

Though it may feel uncomfortable to have multiple records for the same OrderId in the destination table, in this case it's the right thing to do! The goal of data ingestion is to focus on extracting and loading data. What to do with the data is a job for the transform phase of a pipeline, explored in Chapter 6.

Loading Data Extracted from a CDC Log

If your data was extracted via a CDC method, then there is one other consideration. Though it's a similar process to loading data that was extracted incrementally, you'll have access to not only inserted and updated records, but also deleted records.

Take the example of the MySQL binary log extraction from Chapter 4. Recall that the output of the code sample was a CSV file named *orders_extract.csv* that was uploaded to the S3 bucket. Its contents looked like the following:

```
insert|1|Backordered|2020-06-01 12:00:00
update|1|Shipped|2020-06-09 12:00:25
```

Just like the incremental load example earlier in this section, there are two records for OrderId 1. When loaded into the data warehouse, the data looks like it did back in Table 5-1. However, unlike the previous example, *orders_extract.csv* contains a column for the event responsible for the record in the file. In this example, that's either insert or update. If those were the only two event types, you could ignore the event field and end up with a table in Redshift that looks like Table 5-1. From there, analysts would have access to both records when they build data models later in the pipeline. However, consider another version of *orders_extract.csv* with one more line included:

```
insert|1|Backordered|2020-06-01 12:00:00
update|1|Shipped|2020-06-09 12:00:25
delete|1|Shipped|2020-06-10 9:05:12
```

The third line shows that the order record was deleted the day after it was updated. In a full extraction, the record would have disappeared completely, and an incremental extraction would not have picked up the delete (see "Extracting Data from a MySQL Database" on page 39 for a more detailed explanation). With CDC, however, the delete event was picked up and included in the CSV file.

To accommodate deleted records, it's necessary to add a column to the destination table in the Redshift warehouse to store the event type. Table 5-2 shows what the extended version of the Orders looks like.

Table 5-2. The Orders table with EventType in Redshift

EventType	OrderId	OrderStatus	LastUpdated
insert	1	Backordered	2020-06-01 12:00:00
update	1	Shipped	2020-06-09 12:00:25
delete	1	Shipped	2020-06-10 9:05:12

Once again, the goal of data ingestion in a data pipeline is to efficiently extract data from a source and load it into a destination. The transform step in a pipeline is where the logic to model the data for a specific use case resides. Chapter 6 discusses how to model data loaded via a CDC ingestion, such as this example.

Configuring a Snowflake Warehouse as a Destination

If you're using Snowflake as your data warehouse, you have three options for configuring access to the S3 bucket from your Snowflake instance:

- Configure a Snowflake storage integration
- Configure an AWS IAM role
- Configure an AWS IAM user

Of the three, the first is recommended because of how seamless using a Snowflake storage integration is when later interacting with the S3 bucket from Snowflake. Because the specifics of the configuration include a number of steps, it's best to refer to the latest Snowflake documentation (*https://oreil.ly/RCoMT*) on the topic.

In the final step of the configuration you'll create an *external stage*. An external stage is an object that points to an external storage location so Snowflake can access it. The S3 bucket you created earlier will serve as that location.

Before you create the stage, it's handy to define a FILE FORMAT in Snowflake that you can both refer to for the stage and later use for similar file formats. Because the examples in this chapter create pipe-delimited CSV files, create the following FILE FORMAT:

```
CREATE or REPLACE FILE FORMAT pipe_csv_format
TYPE = 'csv'
FIELD_DELIMITER = '|';
```

When you create the stage for the bucket per the final step of the Snowflake documentation, the syntax will look something like this:

```
USE SCHEMA my_db.my_schema;

CREATE STAGE my_s3_stage
  storage_integration = s3_int
  url = 's3://pipeline-bucket/'
  file_format = pipe_csv_format;
```

In "Loading Data into a Snowflake Data Warehouse" on page 97, you'll be using the stage to load data that's been extracted and stored in the S3 bucket into Snowflake.

Finally, you'll need to add a section to the *pipeline.conf* file with Snowflake login credentials. Note that the user you specify must have USAGE permission on the stage you just created. Also, the account_name value must be formatted based on your cloud provider and the region where the account is located. For

---

example, if your account is named `snowflake_acct1` and hosted in the US East (Ohio) region of AWS, the `account_name` value will be `snowflake_acct1.us-east-2.aws`. Because this value will be used to connect to Snowflake via Python using the `snowflake-connector-python` library, you can refer to the library documentation (*https://oreil.ly/ijcHw*) for help determining the proper value for your `account_name`.

Here is the section to add to *pipeline.conf*:

```
[snowflake_creds]
username = snowflake_user
password = snowflake_password
account_name = snowflake_acct1.us-east-2.aws
```

Loading Data into a Snowflake Data Warehouse

Loading data into Snowflake follows a nearly identical pattern to the previous sections on loading data into Redshift. As such, I will not discuss the specifics of handing full, incremental, or CDC data extracts. Rather, I will describe the syntax of loading data from a file that has been extracted.

The mechanism for loading data into Snowflake is the `COPY INTO` command. `COPY INTO` loads the contents of a file or multiple files into a table in the Snowflake warehouse. You can read more about the advanced usage and options of the command in the Snowflake documentation (*https://oreil.ly/E3KG5*).

NOTE

Snowflake also has a data integration service called *Snowpipe* that enables loading data from files as soon as they're available in a Snowflake stage like the one used in the example in this section. You can use Snowpipe to continuously load data rather than scheduling a bulk load via the `COPY INTO` command.

Each extraction example in Chapter 4 wrote a CSV file to an S3 bucket. In "Configuring a Snowflake Warehouse as a Destination" on page 95, you created a Snowflake stage called my_s3_stage that is linked to that bucket. Now, using the COPY INTO command, you can load the file into a Snowflake table as follows:

```
COPY INTO destination_table
  FROM @my_s3_stage/extract_file.csv;
```

It's also possible to load multiple files into the table at once. In some cases, data is extracted into more than one file due to volume or as a result of multiple extraction job runs since the last load. If the files have a consistent naming pattern (and they should!), you can load them all using the pattern parameter:

```
COPY INTO destination_table
  FROM @my_s3_stage
  pattern='.*extract.*.csv';
```

NOTE

The format of the file to be loaded was set when you created the Snowflake stage (a pipe-delimited CSV); thus, you do not need to state it in the COPY INTO command syntax.

Now that you know how the COPY INTO command works, it's time to write a short Python script that can be scheduled and executed to automate the load in a pipeline. See Chapter 7 for more details on this and other pipeline orchestration techniques.

First, you'll need to install a Python library to connect to your Snowflake instance. You can do so using pip:

```
(env) $ pip install snowflake-connector-python
```

Now, you can write a simple Python script to connect to your Snowflake instance and use `COPY INTO` to load the contents of the CSV file into a destination table:

```python
import snowflake.connector
import configparser

parser = configparser.ConfigParser()
parser.read("pipeline.conf")
username = parser.get("snowflake_creds",
            "username")
password =  parser.get("snowflake_creds",
            "password")
account_name = parser.get("snowflake_creds",
            "account_name")

snow_conn = snowflake.connector.connect(
    user = username,
    password = password,
    account = account_name
    )

sql = """COPY INTO destination_table
  FROM @my_s3_stage
  pattern='.*extract.*.csv';"""

cur = snow_conn.cursor()
cur.execute(sql)
cur.close()
```

Using Your File Storage as a Data Lake

There are times when it makes sense to extract data from an S3 bucket (or other cloud storage) and not load into a data warehouse. Data stored in a structured or semistructured form in this way is often referred to as a *data lake*.

Unlike a data warehouse, a data lake stores data in many formats in a raw and sometimes unstructured form. It's cheaper to store, but is not optimized for querying in the same way that structured data in a warehouse is.

However, in recent years, tools have come along to make querying data in a data lake far more accessible and often transparent to a user comfortable with SQL. For example, Amazon Athena is an AWS service that allows a user to query data stored in S3 using SQL. Amazon Redshift Spectrum is a service that allows Redshift to access data in S3 as an *external table* and reference it in queries alongside tables in the Redshift warehouse. Other cloud providers and products have similar functionality.

When should you consider using such an approach rather than structuring and loading the data into your warehouse? There are a few situations that stand out.

Storing large amounts of data in a cloud storage–based data lake is less expensive than storing it in a warehouse (this is not true for Snowflake data lakes that use the same storage as Snowflake data warehouses). In addition, because it's unstructured or semistructured data (no predefined schema), making changes to the types or properties of data stored is far easier than modifying a warehouse schema. JSON documents are an example of the type of semistructured data that you might encounter in a data lake. If a data structure is frequently changing, you may consider storing it in a data lake, at least for the time being.

During the exploration phase of a data science or machine learning project, the data scientist or machine learning engineer might not know yet exactly what "shape" they need their data in. By granting them access to data in a lake in its raw form, they can explore the data and determine what attributes of the data they need to make use of. Once they know, you can determine whether it makes sense to load the data into a table in the warehouse and gain the query optimization that comes with doing so.

In reality, many organization have both data lakes and data warehouses in their data infrastructure. Over time, the two have become complementary, rather than competing, solutions.

Open Source Frameworks

As you've noticed by now, there are repetitive steps in each data ingestion (both in the extract and load steps). As such, numerous frameworks that provide the core functionally and connections to common data sources and destinations have sprung up in recent years. Some are open source, as discussed in this section, while the next section provides an overview of some popular commercial products for data ingestions.

One popular open source framework is called Singer (*https://www.singer.io*). Written in Python, Singer uses *taps* to extract data from a source and streams it in JSON to a *target*. For example, if you want to extract data from a MySQL database and load it into a Google BigQuery data warehouse, you'd use the MySQL tap and the BigQuery target.

As with the code samples in this chapter, with Singer you'll still need to use a separate orchestration framework to schedule and coordinate data ingestions (see Chapter 7 for more). However, whether you use Singer or another framework, you have a lot to gain from a well-built foundation to get you up and running quickly.

Being an open source project, there are a wide number of taps and targets available (see some of the most popular in Table 5-3), and you can contribute your own back to the project as well. Singer is well documented and has active Slack (*https://oreil.ly/tBQs0*) and GitHub (*https://oreil.ly/nLJgF*) communities.

Table 5-3. Popular singer taps and targets

Taps	Targets
Google Analytics	CSV
Jira	Google BigQuery
MySQL	PostgreSQL
PostgreSQL	Amazon Redshift
Salesforce	Snowflake

Commercial Alternatives

There are several commercial cloud-hosted products that make many common data ingestions possible without writing a single line of code. They also have built-in scheduling and job orchestration. Of course, this all comes at a cost.

Two of the most popular commercial tools for data ingestion are Stitch (*https://www.stitchdata.com*) and Fivetran (*https://fivetran.com*). Both are fully web-based and accessible to data engineers as well as other data professionals on a data team. They provide hundreds of prebuilt "connectors" to common data sources, such as Salesforce, HubSpot, Google Analytics, GitHub, and more. You can also ingest data from MySQL, Postgres, and other databases. Support for Amazon Redshift, Snowflake, and other data warehouses is built in as well.

If you ingest data from sources that are supported, you'll save a great deal of time in building a new data ingestion. In addition, as Chapter 7 outlines in detail, scheduling and orchestrating data ingestions aren't trivial tasks. With Stitch and Fivetran, you'll be able to build, schedule, and alert on broken ingestion pipelines right in your browser.

Selected connectors on both platforms also support things like job execution timeouts, duplicate data handling, source system schema changes, and more. If you're building ingestions on your own, you'll need to take all that into account yourself.

Of course, there are some trade-offs:

Cost

Both Stitch and Fivetran have volume-based pricing models. Though they differ in how they measure volume and what other features they include in each pricing tier, at the end of the day what you pay is based on how much data you ingest. If you have a number of high-volume data sources to ingest from, it will cost you.

Vendor lock-in

Once you invest in a vendor, you'll be facing a nontrivial amount of work to migrate to another tool or product, should you decide to move on in the future.

Customization requires coding

If the source system you want to ingest from doesn't have a prebuilt connector, you'll have to write a little code on your own. For Stitch, that means writing a custom Singer tap (see the previous section), and with Fivetran, you'll need to write cloud functions using AWS Lambda, Azure Function, or Google Cloud Functions. If you have many custom data sources, such as custom-built REST APIs, you'll end up having to write custom code and then pay for Stitch or Fivetran to run it.

Security and privacy

Though both products serve as passthroughs for your data and don't store it for long periods of time, they still technically have access to both your source systems as well as destinations (usually data warehouses or data lakes). Both Fivetran and Stitch meet high standards for security; however, some organizations are reluctant to utilize them due to risk tolerance, regulatory requirements, potential liability, and the overhead of reviewing and approving a new data processor.

The choice to build or buy is complex and unique to each organization and use case. It's also worth keeping in mind that some organizations use a mix of custom code and a product like

Fivetran or Stitch for data ingestions. For example, it might be most cost effective to write custom code to handle some high-volume ingestions that would be costly to run in a commercial platform but also worth the cost of using Stitch or Fivetran for ingestions with prebuilt, vendor-supported connectors.

If you do choose a mix of custom and commercial tools, keep in mind you'll need to consider how you standardize things such as logging, alerting, and dependency management. Later chapters of this book discuss those subjects and touch on the challenges of managing pipelines that span multiple platforms.

## CHAPTER 6

Transforming Data

In the ELT pattern defined in Chapter 3, once data has been ingested into a data lake or data warehouse (Chapter 4), the next step in a pipeline is data transformation. Data transformation can include both noncontextual manipulation of data and modeling of data with business context and logic in mind.

If the purpose of the pipeline is to produce business insight or analysis, then in addition to any noncontextual transformations, data is further transformed into data models. Recall from Chapter 2 that a data model structures and defines data in a format that is understood and optimized for data analysis. A data model is represented as one or more tables in a data warehouse.

Though data engineers at times build noncontextual transformation in a pipeline, it's become typical for data analysts and analytics engineers to handle the vast majority of data transformations. People in these roles are more empowered than ever thanks to the emergence of the ELT pattern (they have the data they need right in the warehouse!) and supporting tools and frameworks designed with SQL as their primary language.

This chapter explores both noncontextual transformations that are common to nearly every data pipeline as well as data models that power dashboards, reports, and one-time analysis of a business problem. Because SQL is the language of the data analyst and analytics engineer, most transformation code samples are written in SQL. I include a few samples written in Python to illustrate when it makes sense to tightly couple noncontextual transformations to a data ingestion using powerful Python libraries.

As with the data ingestions in Chapters 4 and 5, the code samples are highly simplified and meant as a starting point to more complex transformations. To learn how to run and manage dependencies between transformations and other steps in a pipeline, see Chapter 8.

SQL Compatibility

The SQL queries in this chapter are designed to run on most dialects of SQL. They make use of limited vendor-specific syntax and should run on any modern database that supports SQL with little or no modification.

Noncontextual Transformations

In Chapter 3, I briefly noted the existence of the EtLT sub-pattern, where the lowercase *t* represents some noncontextual data transformations, such as the following:

- Deduplicate records in a table
- Parse URL parameters into individual components

Though there are countless examples, by providing code samples for these transformations I hope to cover some common patterns of noncontextual transformations. The next section talks about when it makes sense to perform these transformations as part of data ingestion (EtLT) versus post-ingestion (ELT).

Deduplicating Records in a Table

Though not ideal, it is possible for duplicate records to exist in a table of data that has been ingested into a data warehouse. There are a number of reasons it happens:

- An incremental data ingestion mistakenly overlaps a previous ingestion time window and picks up some records that were already ingested in a previous run.

- Duplicate records were inadvertently created in a source system.

- Data that was backfilled overlapped with subsequent data loaded into the table during ingestion.

Whatever the reason, checking for and removing duplicate records is best performed using SQL queries. Each of the following SQL queries refers to the Orders table in a database shown in Table 6-1. The table contains five records, two of which are duplicates. Though there are three records for OrderId 1, the second and fourth rows are exactly the same. The goal of this example is to identify this duplication and resolve it. Though this example has two records that are exactly the same, the logic in the following code samples is valid if there are three, four or even more copies of the same record in the table.

Table 6-1. Orders table with duplicates

OrderId	OrderStatus	LastUpdated
1	Backordered	2020-06-01
1	Shipped	2020-06-09
2	Shipped	2020-07-11
1	Shipped	2020-06-09
3	Shipped	2020-07-12

If you'd like to create a populate such an Orders table for use in Examples 6-1 and 6-2, here is the SQL to do so:

```
CREATE TABLE Orders (
  OrderId int,
  OrderStatus varchar(30),
  LastUpdated timestamp
);

INSERT INTO Orders
  VALUES(1,'Backordered', '2020-06-01');
INSERT INTO Orders
  VALUES(1,'Shipped', '2020-06-09');
INSERT INTO Orders
  VALUES(2,'Shipped', '2020-07-11');
INSERT INTO Orders
  VALUES(1,'Shipped', '2020-06-09');
INSERT INTO Orders
  VALUES(3,'Shipped', '2020-07-12');
```

Identifying duplicate records in a table is simple. You can use the GROUP BY and HAVING statements in SQL. The following query returns any duplicate records along with a count of how many there are:

```
SELECT OrderId,
  OrderStatus,
  LastUpdated,
  COUNT(*) AS dup_count
FROM Orders
GROUP BY OrderId, OrderStatus, LastUpdated
HAVING COUNT(*) > 1;
```

When executed, the query returns the following:

```
OrderId | OrderStatus | LastUpdated | dup_count
1       | Shipped     | 2020-06-09  | 2
```

Now that you know that at least one duplicate exists, you can remove the duplicate records. I'm going to cover two ways to do so. The method you choose depends on many factors related

---

to the optimization of your database as well as your preference in SQL syntax. I suggest trying both and comparing runtimes.

The first method is to use a sequence of queries. The first query creates a copy of the table from the original using the DISTINCT statement. The result of the first query is a result set with only four rows, since the two duplicate rows are turned into one thanks to DISTINCT. Next, the original table is truncated. Finally, the deduplicated version of the dataset is inserted into the original table, as shown in Example 6-1.

Example 6-1. distinct_orders_1.sql

```
CREATE TABLE distinct_orders AS
SELECT DISTINCT OrderId,
  OrderStatus,
  LastUpdated
FROM ORDERS;

TRUNCATE TABLE Orders;

INSERT INTO Orders
SELECT * FROM distinct_orders;

DROP TABLE distinct_orders;
```

WARNING

After the TRUNCATE operation on the Orders table, the table will be empty until the following INSERT operation is complete. During that time, the Orders table is empty and essentially not accessible by any user or process that queries it. While the INSERT operation may not take long, for very large tables you may consider dropping the Orders table and then renaming distinct_orders to Orders instead.

Another approach is to use a *window function* to group duplicate rows and assign them row numbers to identify which ones to delete and which one to keep. I'll use the ROW_NUMBER function to rank the records, and the PARTITION BY statement to group the records by each column. By doing this, any group of records with more than one match (our duplicates) will get assigned a ROW_NUMBER greater than 1.

If you executed Example 6-1, please make sure to refresh the Orders table using the INSERT statements from earlier in this section so that it again contains what is shown in Table 6-1. You'll want to have a duplicate row to work with for the following sample!

Here is what happens when such a query is run on the Orders table:

```
SELECT OrderId,
   OrderStatus,
   LastUpdated,
   ROW_NUMBER() OVER(PARTITION BY OrderId,
                     OrderStatus,
                     LastUpdated)
      AS dup_count
FROM Orders;
```

The result of the query is as follows:

orderid	orderstatus	lastupdated	dup_count
1	Backordered	2020-06-01	1
1	Shipped	2020-06-09	1
1	Shipped	2020-06-09	2
2	Shipped	2020-07-11	1
3	Shipped	2020-07-12	1

As you can see, the third row in the result set has a dup_count value of 2, as it is a duplicate of the record right above it. Now, just like the first approach, you can create a table with the deduplicated records, truncate the Orders table, and finally insert the cleaned dataset into Orders. Example 6-2 shows the full source.

Example 6-2. distinct_orders_2.sql

```sql
CREATE TABLE all_orders AS
SELECT
  OrderId,
  OrderStatus,
  LastUpdated,
  ROW_NUMBER() OVER(PARTITION BY OrderId,
                    OrderStatus,
                    LastUpdated)
    AS dup_count
FROM Orders;

TRUNCATE TABLE Orders;

-- only insert non-duplicated records
INSERT INTO Orders
  (OrderId, OrderStatus, LastUpdated)
SELECT
  OrderId,
  OrderStatus,
  LastUpdated
FROM all_orders
WHERE
  dup_count = 1;

DROP TABLE all_orders;
```

Regardless of which approach you take, the result is a deduplicated version of the Orders table, as shown in Table 6-2.

Table 6-2. Orders table without duplicates

OrderId	OrderStatus	LastUpdated
1	Backordered	2020-06-01
1	Shipped	2020-06-09
2	Shipped	2020-07-11
3	Shipped	2020-07-12

Parsing URLs

Parsing out segments of URLs is a task with little or no business context involved. There are a number of URL components that can be parsed out in a transform step and stored in individual columns in a database table.

For example, consider the following URL:

https://www.mydomain.com/page-name?utm_content=textlink&utm_medium=social&utm_source=twitter&utm_campaign=fallsale

There are six components that are valuable and can be parsed and stored into individual columns:

- The domain: *www.domain.com*
- The URL path: */page-name*
- utm_content parameter value: *textlink*
- utm_medium parameter value: *social*
- utm_source parameter value: *twitter*
- utm_campaign parameter value: *fallsale*

UTM Parameters

Urchin Tracking Module (UTM) parameters are URL parameters that are used for tracking marketing and ad campaigns. They are common across most platforms and organizations.

Parsing URLs is possible in both SQL and Python. The time when you're running the transform and where the URLs are stored will help guide your decision on which to use. For example, if you're following an EtLT pattern and can parse the URLs after extraction from a source but before loading into a table in a data warehouse, Python is an excellent option. I will start by providing an example in Python, followed by SQL.

First, install the urllib3 Python library using pip. (See "Setting Up Your Python Environment" on page 34 for instructions on Python configuration):

```
(env) $ pip install urllib3
```

Then, use the urlsplit and parse_qs functions to parse out the relevant components of the URL. In the following code sample, I do so and print out the results:

```
from urllib.parse import urlsplit, parse_qs

url = """https://www.mydomain.com/page-name?utm_con
tent=textlink&utm_medium=social&utm_source=twit
ter&utm_campaign=fallsale"""

split_url = urlsplit(url)
params = parse_qs(split_url.query)

# domain
print(split_url.netloc)

# url path
print(split_url.path)
```

```
# utm parameters
print(params['utm_content'][0])
print(params['utm_medium'][0])
print(params['utm_source'][0])
print(params['utm_campaign'][0])
```

When executed, the code sample produces the following:

```
www.mydomain.com
/page-name
textlink
social
twitter
fallsale
```

As in the data ingestion code samples from Chapters 4 and 5, you can also parse and write out each parameter to a CSV file to be loaded into your data warehouse to complete the ingestion. Example 6-3 contains the code sample that does so for the example URL, but you'll likely be iterating through more than one URL!

Example 6-3. url_parse.sql

```
from urllib.parse import urlsplit, parse_qs
import csv

url = """https://www.mydomain.com/page-name?utm_con
tent=textlink&utm_medium=social&utm_source=twit
ter&utm_campaign=fallsale"""

split_url = urlsplit(url)
params = parse_qs(split_url.query)
parsed_url = []
all_urls = []

# domain
parsed_url.append(split_url.netloc)

# url path
parsed_url.append(split_url.path)
```

```
parsed_url.append(params['utm_content'][0])
parsed_url.append(params['utm_medium'][0])
parsed_url.append(params['utm_source'][0])
parsed_url.append(params['utm_campaign'][0])

all_urls.append(parsed_url)

export_file = "export_file.csv"

with open(export_file, 'w') as fp:
        csvw = csv.writer(fp, delimiter='|')
        csvw.writerows(all_urls)

fp.close()
```

If you need to parse URLs that have already been loaded into the data warehouse using SQL, you may have a more difficult task ahead. Though some data warehouse vendors provide functions to parse URLs, others do not. Snowflake, for instance, provides a function called PARSE_URL that parses a URL into its components and returns the result as a JSON object. For example, if you want to parse the URL in the preceding example, the result will look like this:

```
SELECT parse_url('https://www.mydomain.com/page-
name?utm_content=text
link&utm_medium=social&utm_source=twitter&utm_cam
paign=fallsale');

+--------------------------------------------------
---------------+
| PARSE_URL('https://www.mydomain.com/page-name?
utm_content=textlink&utm_medium=social&utm_source=t
witter&utm_campaign=fallsale') |
|--------------------------------------------------
---------------|
| {                                                |
|     "fragment": null,                            |
|     "host": "www.mydomain.com",                  |
|     "parameters": {                              |
```

```
|    "utm_content": "textlink",  |
|    "utm_medium": "social",     |
|    "utm_source": "twitter",    |
|    "utm_campaign": "fallsale"  |
|  },                            |
|  "path": "/page-name",         |
|  "query":                      
"utm_content=textlink&utm_medium=social&utm_source=
twitter&utm_campaign=fallsale",
                    |
|   "scheme": "HTTPS"            |
| }                              |
+---------------------------------------------------
----------------+
```

If you are using Redshift or another data warehouse platform without built-in URL parsing, you'll need to make use of custom string parsing or regular expressions. For example, Redshift has a function called REGEXP_SUBSTR. Given the difficultly of parsing URLs in most data warehouses, I recommend parsing using Python or another language during data ingestion and loading in the structured URL components.

Save the Original URL!

Whether you parse URLs during data ingestion or afterward, it's best to keep the original URL string in the data warehouse as well. URLs may have a number of parameters that you didn't think to parse out and structure, but will want to access in the future.

When to Transform? During or After Ingestion?

Data transformations without business context, like the ones in the previous section, can be run either during or after data ingestion from a technical standpoint. However, there are some reasons you should consider running them as part of the ingestion process (the EtLT pattern):

1. *The transformation is easiest to do using a language besides SQL*: Like parsing URLs in an earlier example, if you find it's a lot easier to make use of Python libraries to handle the transformation, then do so as part of the data ingestion. In the ELT pattern, transforms done post-ingestion are limited to data modeling that is performed by data analysts who are typically most comfortable in SQL.

2. *The transformation is addressing a data quality issue*: It's best to address data quality as early in a pipeline as possible (Chapter 9 has more detail on this topic). For example, in the previous section I provided an example of identifying and removing duplicate records in data that's been ingested. There's no reason to take the risk of a data analyst getting tripped up by duplicated data if you can catch it and fix it at the point of ingestion. Even though the transform is written in SQL, it can be run at the tail end of the ingestion rather than waiting for the analyst to transform the data.

When it comes to transformations that involve business logic, it's best to keep those separate from data ingestions. As you'll see in the next section, this type of transformation is referred to as *data modeling*.

Data Modeling Foundations

Modeling data for use in analysis, dashboards, and reports is a topic worth dedicating an entire book to. However, there are some principles for modeling data in the ELT pattern that I discuss in this section.

Unlike the previous section, data modeling is where business context is taken into account in the transform step of the ELT pattern in a pipeline. Data models make sense of all the data that's been loaded into the warehouse from various sources during the extract and load steps (data ingestion).

Key Data Modeling Terms

When I use the term *data models* in this section, I'm referring to individual SQL tables in a data warehouse. In the sample data models, I'll focus on two properties of models:

Measures
> These are things you want to measure! Examples include a count of customers and a dollar value of revenue.

Attributes
> These are things by which you want to filter or group in a report or dashboard. Examples include dates, customer names, and countries.

In addition, I will speak to the granularity of a data model. *Granularity* is the level of detail stored in a data model. For example, a model that must provide the number of orders placed each day would require daily granularity. If it had to answer the question of how many orders were placed each hour, then it would require hourly granularity.

Source tables are tables that were loaded into the data warehouse or data lake via a data ingestion as described in Chapters 4 and 5. In data modeling, models are built from both source tables as well as other data models.

Data Model Code Reuse

Though each data model is represented by its own table in a data warehouse, the logic to build it may rely on other data models. To learn more about the benefit of reusing logic and deriving models from one another, see "Reuse of Data Model Logic" on page 218.

Modeling Fully Refreshed Data

When modeling data that has been fully reloaded, such as described in "Extracting Data from a MySQL Database" on page 39, you are confronted with a table (or multiple tables) that contain the latest state of a source data store. For example, Table 6-3 shows records in an Orders table similar to the one in Table 6-2, but with only the latest records rather than a full history. Notice that the Backordered record for OrderId 1 is not present in this version. This is what would be present if the table were loaded in full from the source database to the data warehouse. In other words, it looks like the current state of the Orders table in the source system at the time of data ingestion.

The other differences from Table 6-2 are a fourth column named CustomerId, which stores the identifier of the customer who placed the order, and a fifth column with the OrderTotal, which is the dollar value of the order.

Table 6-3. A fully refreshed Orders table

OrderId	OrderStatus	OrderDate	CustomerId	OrderTotal
1	Shipped	2020-06-09	100	50.05
2	Shipped	2020-07-11	101	57.45
3	Shipped	2020-07-12	102	135.99
4	Shipped	2020-07-12	100	43.00

In addition to the Orders table, consider the Customers table, shown in Table 6-4, which has also been loaded into the warehouse in full (meaning it contains the current state of each customer record).

Table 6-4. A fully refreshed Customers table

CustomerId	CustomerName	CustomerCountry
100	Jane	USA
101	Bob	UK
102	Miles	UK

If you'd like to create these tables in a database for use in the following sections, you can use the following SQL statements to do so. Note that if you created the version of the Orders table in "Deduplicating Records in a Table" on page 107, you'll need to DROP it first.

```sql
CREATE TABLE Orders (
  OrderId int,
  OrderStatus varchar(30),
  OrderDate timestamp,
  CustomerId int,
  OrderTotal numeric
);

INSERT INTO Orders
  VALUES(1,'Shipped','2020-06-09',100,50.05);
INSERT INTO Orders
  VALUES(2,'Shipped','2020-07-11',101,57.45);
INSERT INTO Orders
  VALUES(3,'Shipped','2020-07-12',102,135.99);
INSERT INTO Orders
  VALUES(4,'Shipped','2020-07-12',100,43.00);


CREATE TABLE Customers
(
  CustomerId int,
  CustomerName varchar(20),
  CustomerCountry varchar(10)
);

INSERT INTO Customers VALUES(100,'Jane','USA');
INSERT INTO Customers VALUES(101,'Bob','UK');
INSERT INTO Customers VALUES(102,'Miles','UK');
```

Consider the need to create a data model that can be queried to answer the following questions:

- How much revenue was generated from orders placed from a given country in a given month?
- How many orders were placed on a given day?

Facts and Dimensions

If you're familiar with *dimensional modeling* (sometimes referred to as *Kimball modeling*), you might notice that in this example, the Orders table contains the type of data that would be modeled in a *fact table*, while the data in the Customer table would be modeled in a *dimension*. Such concepts are mostly out of the scope of this book, but if you're a data analyst I highly recommend learning more about the fundamentals of dimensional modeling. For now, I'll be creating a single data model directly from the two source tables.

Though the sample tables contain only a few records, imagine a case where both tables contain millions of records. While answering those questions is quite straightforward using a SQL query, when the data volume is high, query execution time and the volume of data in a model can be reduced if the data model is aggregated to some extent.

If those questions are the only two requirements of the data model, there are two measures it must provide:

- Total Revenue
- Order Count

In addition, there are two attributes which the model must allow a query to filter or group the data by:

- Order Country
- Order Date

Finally, the granularity of the model is daily, since the smallest unit of time in the requirements is by day.

Optimize for Granularity

The number of records in a data model is a factor of the amount of data in the source tables used in the model, the number of attributes, and the granularity. Always pick the granularity of the smallest unit required, but no less. If the model only needs to provide measures by month, then setting daily granularity isn't necessary, and will only increase the number of records your model needs to store and query.

In this highly simplified data model, I'll first define the structure of the model (a SQL table) and then insert the data sourced from a join of both tables:

```
CREATE TABLE IF NOT EXISTS order_summary_daily (
order_date date,
order_country varchar(10),
total_revenue numeric,
order_count int
);

INSERT INTO order_summary_daily
  (order_date, order_country,
  total_revenue, order_count)
SELECT
  o.OrderDate AS order_date,
  c.CustomerCountry AS order_country,
  SUM(o.OrderTotal) as total_revenue,
  COUNT(o.OrderId) AS order_count
FROM Orders o
INNER JOIN Customers c on
  c.CustomerId = o.CustomerId
GROUP BY o.OrderDate, c.CustomerCountry;
```

Now, you can query the model to answer the questions set out in the requirements:

```sql
-- How much revenue was generated from orders
placed from a given country in a given month?

SELECT
  DATE_PART('month', order_date) as order_month,
  order_country,
  SUM(total_revenue) as order_revenue
FROM order_summary_daily
GROUP BY
  DATE_PART('month', order_date),
  order_country
ORDER BY
  DATE_PART('month', order_date),
  order_country;
```

With the sample data from Tables 6-3 and 6-4, the query returns the following results:

```
order_month | order_country | order_revenue
------------+---------------+---------------
          6 | USA           |          50.05
          7 | UK            |         193.44
          7 | USA           |          43.00
(3 rows)
```

```sql
-- How many orders were placed on a given day?
SELECT
  order_date,
  SUM(order_count) as total_orders
FROM order_summary_daily
GROUP BY order_date
ORDER BY order_date;
```

This returns the following:

```
order_date | total_orders
-----------+--------------
2020-06-09 |            1
2020-07-11 |            1
2020-07-12 |            2
(3 rows)
```

Slowly Changing Dimensions for Fully Refreshed Data

Because data that's been ingested as a full refresh overwrites changes to existing data (such as a record in Customers), a more advanced data modeling concept is often implemented to track historical changes.

For example, in the next section you'll make use of a Customers table that's been loaded incrementally and contains updates to CustomerId 100. As you will see in Table 6-6, that customer has a second record indicating that the value of her CustomerCountry changed from "USA" to "UK" on 2020-06-20. That means that when she placed OrderId 4 on 2020-07-12 she no longer lived in the USA.

When analyzing the order history, an analyst might want to allocate a customer's orders to where they lived at the time of an order. With incrementally refreshed data it's a bit easier to do that, as you'll see in the next section. With fully refreshed data, it's necessary to keep a full history of the Customers table between each ingestion and keep track of those changes on your own.

The method for doing so is defined in Kimball (dimensional) modeling and referred to as a *slowly changing dimension* or *SCD*. When dealing with fully refreshed data, I often make use of Type II SCDs, which add a new record to a table for each change to an entity, including the date range that the record was valid.

A Type II SCD with Jane's customer records would look something like Table 6-5. Note that the latest record expires on a date in very distant future. Some Type II SCDs use NULL for unexpired records, but a date far in the future makes querying the table a bit less error prone, as you'll see in a moment.

Table 6-5. A Type II SCD with customer data

CustomerId	CustomerName	CustomerCountry	ValidFrom	Expired
100	Jane	USA	2019-05-01 7:01:10	2020-06-20 8:15:34
100	Jane	UK	2020-06-20 8:15:34	2199-12-31 00:00:00

You can create and populate this table in your database using the following SQL statements:

```
CREATE TABLE Customers_scd
(
  CustomerId int,
  CustomerName varchar(20),
  CustomerCountry varchar(10),
  ValidFrom timestamp,
  Expired timestamp
);

INSERT INTO Customers_scd
  VALUES(100,'Jane','USA','2019-05-01 7:01:10',
    '2020-06-20 8:15:34');
INSERT INTO Customers_scd
  VALUES(100,'Jane','UK','2020-06-20 8:15:34',
    '2199-12-31 00:00:00');
```

You can join the SCD with the Orders table you created earlier to get the properties of the customer record at the time of the order. To do so, in addition to joining on the CustomerId, you'll also need to join on the date range in the SCD that the order was placed in. For example, this query will return the country that Jane's Customers_scd record indicated she lived in at the time each of her orders was placed:

```
SELECT
  o.OrderId,
  o.OrderDate,
  c.CustomerName,
  c.CustomerCountry
FROM Orders o
```

```
INNER JOIN Customers_scd c
  ON o.CustomerId = c.CustomerId
    AND o.OrderDate BETWEEN c.ValidFrom AND
c.Expired
ORDER BY o.OrderDate;
```

```
orderid |      orderdate      | customer | customer
                              |   name   |  country
--------+---------------------+----------+---------
      1 | 2020-06-09 00:00:00 | Jane     | USA
      4 | 2020-07-12 00:00:00 | Jane     | UK
(2 rows)
```

Though this logic is all you need to make use of SCDs in data modeling, keeping SCDs up to date can be a challenge. In the case of the Customers table, you'll need to take a snapshot of it after each ingestion and look for any CustomerId records that have changed. The best approach for doing so depends on which data warehouse and which data orchestration tools you are using. If you are interested in implementing SCDs, I suggest learning the fundamentals of Kimball modeling, which is outside the scope of this book. For more in-depth reading on the subject, I suggest the book *The Data Warehouse Toolkit*, by Ralph Kimball and Margy Ross (Wiley, 2013).

Modeling Incrementally Ingested Data

Recall from Chapter 4 that data ingested incrementally contains not only the current state of the source data, but also historical records from since the ingestion started. For example, consider the same Orders table as in the prior section, but with a new customers table named Customers_staging that is ingested incrementally. As you can see in Table 6-6, there are new columns for the UpdatedDate value of the record, as well as a new record for CustomerId 100 indicating that Jane's Customer Country (where she lives) changed from the US to the UK on 2020-06-20.

Table 6-6. The incrementally loaded Customers_staging table

CustomerId	CustomerName	CustomerCountry	LastUpdated
100	Jane	USA	2019-05-01 7:01:10
101	Bob	UK	2020-01-15 13:05:31
102	Miles	UK	2020-01-29 9:12:00
100	Jane	UK	2020-06-20 8:15:34

You can create and populate the Customers_staging table in your database for use in the following examples using these SQL statements:

```
CREATE TABLE Customers_staging (
  CustomerId int,
  CustomerName varchar(20),
  CustomerCountry varchar(10),
  LastUpdated timestamp
);

INSERT INTO Customers_staging
  VALUES(100,'Jane','USA','2019-05-01 7:01:10');
INSERT INTO Customers_staging
  VALUES(101,'Bob','UK','2020-01-15 13:05:31');
INSERT INTO Customers_staging
  VALUES(102,'Miles','UK','2020-01-29 9:12:00');
INSERT INTO Customers_staging
  VALUES(100,'Jane','UK','2020-06-20 8:15:34');
```

Recall the questions the model needs to answer from the previous section, which I'll apply to the model in this section as well:

- How much revenue was generated from orders placed from a given country in a given month?

- How many orders were placed on a given day?

Before you can build your data model in this case, you'll need to decide how you want to handle changes to records in the Customer table. In the example of Jane, which country should her two orders in the Orders table be allocated to? Should they both be allocated to her current country (UK) or each to the country that she lived in at the time of the order (the US and the UK respectively)?

The choice you make is based on the logic required by the business case, but the implementation of each is a bit different. I'll start with an example of allocating to her current country. I'll do this by building a data model similar to the one in the previous section, but using only the most current record for each CustomerId in the Customers_staging table. Note that because the second question in the requirements for the model requires daily granularity, I'll build the model at the date level:

```
CREATE TABLE order_summary_daily_current
(
  order_date date,
  order_country varchar(10),
  total_revenue numeric,
  order_count int
);

INSERT INTO order_summary_daily_current
  (order_date, order_country,
  total_revenue, order_count)
WITH customers_current AS
(
  SELECT CustomerId,
    MAX(LastUpdated) AS latest_update
  FROM Customers_staging
  GROUP BY CustomerId
)
SELECT
  o.OrderDate AS order_date,
  cs.CustomerCountry AS order_country,
  SUM(o.OrderTotal) AS total_revenue,
  COUNT(o.OrderId) AS order_count
FROM Orders o
INNER JOIN customers_current cc
  ON cc.CustomerId = o.CustomerId
INNER JOIN Customers_staging cs
  ON cs.CustomerId = cc.CustomerId
```

```
     AND cs.LastUpdated = cc.latest_update
  GROUP BY o.OrderDate, cs.CustomerCountry;
```

When answering the question of how much revenue was generated from orders placed in a given country in a given month, both of Jane's orders are allocated to the UK, even though you might expect to see the 50.05 from her order in June to be allocated to the US, given that's where she lived at the time:

```
SELECT
  DATE_PART('month', order_date) AS order_month,
  order_country,
  SUM(total_revenue) AS order_revenue
FROM order_summary_daily_current
GROUP BY
  DATE_PART('month', order_date),
  order_country
ORDER BY
  DATE_PART('month', order_date),
  order_country;

order_month | order_country | order_revenue
------------+---------------+---------------
          6 | UK            |         50.05
          7 | UK            |        236.44
(2 rows)
```

If instead you want to allocate orders to the country that the customers lived in at the time of order, then building the model requires a change in logic. Instead of finding the most recent record in Customers_staging for each CustomerId in the *common table expression* (CTE), I instead find the most recent record that was updated on or before the time of each order placed by each customer. In other words, I want the information about the customer that was valid at the time they placed the order. That information is stored in the version of their Customer_staging record when the order was placed. Any later updates to their customer information didn't occur until after that particular order was placed.

The customer_pit (*pit* is short for "point-in-time") CTE in the following sample contains the MAX(cs.LastUpdated) for each CustomerId/OrderId pair. I use that information in the final SELECT statement to populate the data model. Note that I must join based on both the OrderId and CustomerId in this query. Here is the final SQL for the order_summary_daily_pit model:

```
CREATE TABLE order_summary_daily_pit
(
  order_date date,
  order_country varchar(10),
  total_revenue numeric,
  order_count int
);

INSERT INTO order_summary_daily_pit
  (order_date, order_country, total_revenue,
order_count)
WITH customer_pit AS
(
  SELECT
    cs.CustomerId,
    o.OrderId,
    MAX(cs.LastUpdated) AS max_update_date
  FROM Orders o
  INNER JOIN Customers_staging cs
    ON cs.CustomerId = o.CustomerId
      AND cs.LastUpdated <= o.OrderDate
  GROUP BY cs.CustomerId, o.OrderId
)
SELECT
  o.OrderDate AS order_date,
  cs.CustomerCountry AS order_country,
  SUM(o.OrderTotal) AS total_revenue,
  COUNT(o.OrderId) AS order_count
FROM Orders o
INNER JOIN customer_pit cp
  ON cp.CustomerId = o.CustomerId
    AND cp.OrderId = o.OrderId
INNER JOIN Customers_staging cs
```

```
   ON cs.CustomerId = cp.CustomerId
     AND cs.LastUpdated = cp.max_update_date
 GROUP BY o.OrderDate, cs.CustomerCountry;
```

When you run the same query as before, you'll see that the revenue from Jane's first order is allocated to the US in June 2020,
while the second order in July 2020 remains allocated to the
UK as expected:

```
SELECT
  DATE_PART('month', order_date) AS order_month,
  order_country,
  SUM(total_revenue) AS order_revenue
FROM order_summary_daily_pit
GROUP BY
  DATE_PART('month', order_date),
  order_country
ORDER BY
  DATE_PART('month', order_date),
  order_country;

order_month | order_country | order_revenue
------------+---------------+---------------
          6 | USA           |         50.05
          7 | UK            |        236.44
(2 rows)
```

Modeling Append-Only Data

Append-only data (or *insert-only data*) is immutable data that is
ingested into a data warehouse. Each record in such a table is
some kind of event that never changes. An example is a table of
all page views on a website. Each time the data ingestion runs,
it appends new page views to the table but never updates or
deletes previous events. What occurred in the past happened
and cannot be changed.

Modeling append-only data is similar to modeling fully
refreshed data. However, you can optimize the creation and
refresh of data models built off of such data by taking advan-

tage of the fact that once records are inserted, they'll never change.

Table 6-7 is an example of an append-only table named Page Views containing record page views on a website. Each record in the table represents a customer viewing a page on a company's website. New records, representing page views logged since the last ingestion, are appended to the table each time the data ingestion job runs.

Table 6-7. PageViews table

CustomerId	ViewTime	UrlPath	utm_medium
100	2020-06-01 12:00:00	/home	social
100	2020-06-01 12:00:13	/product/2554	NULL
101	2020-06-01 12:01:30	/product/6754	search
102	2020-06-02 7:05:00	/home	NULL
101	2020-06-02 12:00:00	/product/2554	social

You can create and populate the PageViews table in your database for use in the following examples using these SQL queries.

```
CREATE TABLE PageViews (
  CustomerId int,
  ViewTime timestamp,
  UrlPath varchar(250),
  utm_medium varchar(50)
);

INSERT INTO PageViews
  VALUES(100,'2020-06-01 12:00:00',
    '/home','social');
INSERT INTO PageViews
  VALUES(100,'2020-06-01 12:00:13',
    '/product/2554',NULL);
INSERT INTO PageViews
  VALUES(101,'2020-06-01 12:01:30',
    '/product/6754','search');
INSERT INTO PageViews
```

```
        VALUES(102,'2020-06-02 7:05:00',
          '/home','NULL');
    INSERT INTO PageViews
      VALUES(101,'2020-06-02 12:00:00',
        '/product/2554','social');
```

Note that a real table with page view data would contain dozens or more columns storing attributes about the page viewed, the referring URL, the user's browser version, and more.

Recall URL Parsing

The PageViews table in Table 6-7 is a good example of the type of table that is created via the methods described in "Parsing URLs" on page 112.

Now, I'll define a data model that is designed to answer the following questions. I'll be using the Customers table defined in Table 6-4 earlier in this chapter to identify the country that each customer resides in:

- How many page views are there for each UrlPath on the site by day?
- How many page views do customers from each country generate each day?

The granularity of the data model is daily. There are three attributes required.

- The date (no timestamp required) of the page view
- The UrlPath of the page view
- The country that the customer viewing the page resides in

There is only one metric required:

- A count of page views

The structure of the model is as follows:

```
CREATE TABLE pageviews_daily (
  view_date date,
  url_path varchar(250),
  customer_country varchar(50),
  view_count int
);
```

To populate the model for the first time, the logic is the same as in the "Modeling Fully Refreshed Data" section of this chapter. All records from the PageViews table are included in the population of pageviews_daily. Example 6-4 shows the SQL.

Example 6-4. pageviews_daily.sql

```
INSERT INTO pageviews_daily
  (view_date, url_path, customer_country, view_count)
SELECT
  CAST(p.ViewTime as Date) AS view_date,
  p.UrlPath AS url_path,
  c.CustomerCountry AS customer_country,
  COUNT(*) AS view_count
FROM PageViews p
LEFT JOIN Customers c ON c.CustomerId = p.CustomerId
GROUP BY
  CAST(p.ViewTime as Date),
  p.UrlPath,
  c.CustomerCountry;
```

To answer one of the questions required by the model (how many page views do customers from each country generate each day?), the following SQL will do the trick:

```
SELECT
  view_date,
  customer_country,
  SUM(view_count)
FROM pageviews_daily
GROUP BY view_date, customer_country
ORDER BY view_date, customer_country;
```

```
view_date    | customer_country | sum
-------------+------------------+-----
2020-06-01 | UK               |   1
2020-06-01 | USA              |   2
2020-06-02 | UK               |   2
(3 rows)
```

Now consider what to do when the next ingestion of data into the PageViews table runs. New records are added, but all existing records remain untouched. To update the pageviews_daily model, you have two options:

- Truncate the pageviews_daily table and run the same INSERT statement you used to populate it for the first time. In this case, you are *fully refreshing* the model.

- Only load new records from PageViews into page views_daily. In this case, you are *incrementally refreshing* the model.

The first option is the least complex and less likely to result in any logical errors on the part of the analyst building the model. If the INSERT operation runs quickly enough for your use case, then I suggest taking this path. Beware, however! While the full refresh of the model might run quickly enough when it's first developed, as the PageViews and Customers datasets grow, the runtime of the refresh will grow as well.

The second option is a little more complicated but may result in a shorter runtime when you're working with larger datasets. The tricky part of an incremental refresh in this case is the fact that the pageviews_daily table is granular to the day (date with no timestamp), while new records ingested into the PageViews table are granular to a full timestamp.

Why is that a problem? It's unlikely that you refreshed page views_daily at the end of a full day of records. In other words, though pageviews_daily has data for 2020-06-02, it's possible that new records for that day will be loaded into PageViews in the next ingestion run.

Table 6-8 shows just that case. Two new records have been appended to the previous version of PageViews from Table 6-7. The first of the new page views occurred on 2020-06-02, and the second was on the following day.

Table 6-8. PageViews table with additional records

CustomerId	ViewTime	UrlPath	utm_medium
100	2020-06-01 12:00:00	/home	social
100	2020-06-01 12:00:13	/product/2554	NULL
101	2020-06-01 12:01:30	/product/6754	search
102	2020-06-02 7:05:00	/home	NULL
101	2020-06-02 12:00:00	/product/2554	social
102	2020-06-02 12:03:42	/home	NULL
101	2020-06-03 12:25:01	/product/567	social

Before I attempt to incremental refresh the pageviews_daily model, take a look at a snapshot of what it looks like currently:

```
SELECT *
FROM pageviews_daily
ORDER BY view_date, url_path, customer_country;

view_date   |   url_path     | customer | view_count
                              | _country
------------+----------------+----------+----------
2020-06-01  | /home          | USA      |    1
2020-06-01  | /product/2554  | USA      |    1
2020-06-01  | /product/6754  | UK       |    1
2020-06-02  | /home          | UK       |    1
2020-06-02  | /product/2554  | UK       |    1
(5 rows)
```

You can now insert the two new records shown in Table 6-8 into your database using the following SQL statements:

```
INSERT INTO PageViews
  VALUES(102,'2020-06-02 12:03:42',
    '/home',NULL);
```

```
INSERT INTO PageViews
  VALUES(101,'2020-06-03 12:25:01',
    '/product/567','social');
```

As a first attempt at an incremental refresh, you might simply include records from PageViews with a timestamp greater than the current MAX(view_date) in pageviews_daily (2020-06-02) into pageviews_daily. I'll try that, but instead of inserting into pageviews_daily, I'll create another copy of it called page views_daily_2 and use that for this example. Why? Well, as you'll see in a moment, this is not the correct approach! The SQL would look like the following:

```
CREATE TABLE pageviews_daily_2 AS
SELECT * FROM pageviews_daily;

INSERT INTO pageviews_daily_2
  (view_date, url_path,
  customer_country, view_count)
SELECT
  CAST(p.ViewTime as Date) AS view_date,
  p.UrlPath AS url_path,
  c.CustomerCountry AS customer_country,
  COUNT(*) AS view_count
FROM PageViews p
LEFT JOIN Customers c
  ON c.CustomerId = p.CustomerId
WHERE
  p.ViewTime >
  (SELECT MAX(view_date) FROM pageviews_daily_2)
GROUP BY
  CAST(p.ViewTime as Date),
  p.UrlPath,
  c.CustomerCountry;
```

However, as you can see in the following code, you'll end up with several duplicate records because all events from 2020-06-02 at midnight and after are included in the refresh. In other words, page views from 2020-06-02 that were previously accounted for in the model are counted again. That's because we don't have the full timestamp stored in the daily granular pageviews_daily (and the copy named pageviews_daily_2). If this version of the model was used for reporting or analysis, the number of page views would be overstated!

```
SELECT *
FROM pageviews_daily_2
ORDER BY view_date, url_path, customer_country;
```

view_date	url_path	customer _country	view_count
2020-06-01	/home	USA	1
2020-06-01	/product/2554	USA	1
2020-06-01	/product/6754	UK	1
2020-06-02	/home	UK	2
2020-06-02	/home	UK	1
2020-06-02	/product/2554	UK	1
2020-06-02	/product/2554	UK	1
2020-06-03	/product/567	UK	1

(8 rows)

If you sum up view_count by date, you'll see that there are five page views on 2020-06-02 instead of the actual count of three from Table 6-8. That's because the two page views from that day that were previously added to pageviews_daily_2 were added again:

```
SELECT
  view_date,
  SUM(view_count) AS daily_views
FROM pageviews_daily_2
GROUP BY view_date
ORDER BY view_date;
```

view_date	daily_views
2020-06-01	3
2020-06-02	5
2020-06-03	1

(3 rows)

Another approach that many analysts take is to store the full timestamp of the final record from the PageViews table and use it as the next starting point for the incremental refresh. Like last time, I'll create a new table (this time called page views_daily_3) for this attempt as it is the incorrect solution:

```
CREATE TABLE pageviews_daily_3 AS
SELECT * FROM pageviews_daily;

INSERT INTO pageviews_daily_3
  (view_date, url_path,
  customer_country, view_count)
SELECT
  CAST(p.ViewTime as Date) AS view_date,
  p.UrlPath AS url_path,
  c.CustomerCountry AS customer_country,
  COUNT(*) AS view_count
FROM PageViews p
LEFT JOIN Customers c
  ON c.CustomerId = p.CustomerId
WHERE p.ViewTime > '2020-06-02 12:00:00'
GROUP BY
  CAST(p.ViewTime AS Date),
  p.UrlPath,
  c.CustomerCountry;
```

Again, if you take a look at the new version of page views_daily_3, you'll notice something nonideal. Although the total number of page views for 2020-06-02 is now correct (3), there are two rows that are the same (view_date of 2020-06-02, url_path of /home, and customer_country of UK):

```
SELECT *
FROM pageviews_daily_3
ORDER BY view_date, url_path, customer_country;
```

view_date	url_path	customer_country	view_count
2020-06-01	/home	USA	1
2020-06-01	/product/2554	USA	1

```
2020-06-01 | /product/6754 | UK    |    1
2020-06-02 | /home         | UK    |    1
2020-06-02 | /home         | UK    |    1
2020-06-02 | /product/2554 | UK    |    1
2020-06-03 | /product/567  | UK    |    1
(7 rows)
```

Thankfully, in this case, the answer to the question of how many page views there are by day and country is correct. However, it's wasteful to store data we don't need. Those two records could have been combined into a single one with a `view_count` value of 2. Though the sample table is small in this case, it's not uncommon for such tables to have many billion records in reality. The number of unnecessary duplicated records add up and wastes storage and future query time.

A better approach is to assume that more data has been loaded during the latest day (or week, month, and so on, based on the granularity of the table) in the model. The approach I'll take is as follows:

1. Make a copy of `pageviews_daily` called `tmp_page views_daily` with all records up through the second to last day that it currently contains. In this example, that means all data through 2020-06-01.

2. Insert all records from the source table (`PageViews`) into the copy starting on the next day (2020-06-02).

3. Truncate `pageviews_daily` and load the data from `tmp_pageviews_daily` into it.

4. Drop `tmp_pageviews_daily`.

A Modified Approach

Some analysts prefer to take a slightly different approach. Instead of truncating `pageviews_daily` in step 3, they instead drop `pageviews_daily` and then rename `tmp_pageviews_daily` to `pageviews_daily`. The upside is that `pageviews_daily` isn't

---

empty between steps 3 and 4 and can be queried right away. The downside is that on some data warehouse platforms you'll lose permissions set on pageviews_daily if they were not copied over to tmp_pageviews_daily in step 1. Consult the documentation for your data warehouse platform before considering this alternate approach.

The final, and correct, SQL for the incremental refresh of the model is as follows:

```sql
CREATE TABLE tmp_pageviews_daily AS
SELECT *
FROM pageviews_daily
WHERE view_date
  < (SELECT MAX(view_date) FROM pageviews_daily);

INSERT INTO tmp_pageviews_daily
  (view_date, url_path,
  customer_country, view_count)
SELECT
  CAST(p.ViewTime as Date) AS view_date,
  p.UrlPath AS url_path,
  c.CustomerCountry AS customer_country,
  COUNT(*) AS view_count
FROM PageViews p
LEFT JOIN Customers c
  ON c.CustomerId = p.CustomerId
WHERE p.ViewTime
  > (SELECT MAX(view_date) FROM pageviews_daily)
GROUP BY
  CAST(p.ViewTime as Date),
  p.UrlPath,
  c.CustomerCountry;

TRUNCATE TABLE pageviews_daily;

INSERT INTO pageviews_daily
SELECT * FROM tmp_pageviews_daily;

DROP TABLE tmp_pageviews_daily;
```

Finally, the following is the result of the proper incremental refresh. The total count of page views is correct, and the data is stored as efficiently as possible, given the requirements of the model:

```
SELECT *
FROM pageviews_daily
ORDER BY view_date, url_path, customer_country;

view_date   |   url_path    | customer | view_count
                            | _country
------------+---------------+----------+-----------
2020-06-01  | /home         | USA      |     1
2020-06-01  | /product/2554 | USA      |     1
2020-06-01  | /product/6754 | UK       |     1
2020-06-02  | /home         | UK       |     2
2020-06-02  | /product/2554 | UK       |     1
2020-06-03  | /product/567  | UK       |     1
(6 rows)
```

Modeling Change Capture Data

Recall from Chapter 4 that data ingested via CDC is stored in a specific way in the data warehouse after ingestion. For example, Table 6-9 shows the contents of a table named Orders_cdc that's been ingested via CDC. It contains the history of three orders in a source system.

Table 6-9. The Orders_cdc table

EventType	OrderId	OrderStatus	LastUpdated
insert	1	Backordered	2020-06-01 12:00:00
update	1	Shipped	2020-06-09 12:00:25
delete	1	Shipped	2020-06-10 9:05:12
insert	2	Backordered	2020-07-01 11:00:00
update	2	Shipped	2020-07-09 12:15:12
insert	3	Backordered	2020-07-11 13:10:12

You can create and populate the Orders_cdc table with the following SQL statements:

```sql
CREATE TABLE Orders_cdc
(
  EventType varchar(20),
  OrderId int,
  OrderStatus varchar(20),
  LastUpdated timestamp
);

INSERT INTO Orders_cdc
  VALUES('insert',1,'Backordered',
    '2020-06-01 12:00:00');
INSERT INTO Orders_cdc
  VALUES('update',1,'Shipped',
    '2020-06-09 12:00:25');
INSERT INTO Orders_cdc
  VALUES('delete',1,'Shipped',
    '2020-06-10 9:05:12');
INSERT INTO Orders_cdc
  VALUES('insert',2,'Backordered',
    '2020-07-01 11:00:00');
INSERT INTO Orders_cdc
  VALUES('update',2,'Shipped',
    '2020-07-09 12:15:12');
INSERT INTO Orders_cdc
  VALUES('insert',3,'Backordered',
    '2020-07-11 13:10:12');
```

Order 1's record was first created when the order was placed, but in a status of Backordered. Eight days later, the record was updated in the source system when it shipped. A day later the record was deleted in the source system for some reason. Order 2 took a similar journey but was never deleted. Order 3 was first inserted when it was placed and has never been updated. Thanks to CDC, we not only know the current state of all orders, but also their full history.

How to model data stored in this way depends on what questions the data model sets out to answer. For example, you might want to report on the current status of all orders for use on an operational dashboard. Perhaps the dashboard needs to display the number of orders currently in each state. A simple model would look something like this:

```sql
CREATE TABLE orders_current (
  order_status varchar(20),
  order_count int
);

INSERT INTO orders_current
  (order_status, order_count)
  WITH o_latest AS
  (
    SELECT
      OrderId,
      MAX(LastUpdated) AS max_updated
    FROM Orders_cdc
    GROUP BY orderid
  )
  SELECT o.OrderStatus,
    Count(*) as order_count
  FROM Orders_cdc o
  INNER JOIN o_latest
    ON o_latest.OrderId = o_latest.OrderId
      AND o_latest.max_updated = o.LastUpdated
  GROUP BY o.OrderStatus;
```

In this example, I use a CTE instead of a subquery to find the MAX(LastUpdated) timestamp for each OrderId. I then join the resulting CTE to the Orders_cdc table to get the OrderStatus of the most recent record for each order.

To answer the original question, you can see that two orders have an OrderStatus of Shipped and one is still Backordered:

```sql
SELECT * FROM orders_current;

order_status | order_count
-------------+-------------
Shipped      |           2
```

```
Backordered  |              1
(2 rows)
```

Is this the right answer to the question, however? Recall that while the latest status of OrderId 1 was currently Shipped, the Order record was deleted from the source database. Though that may seem like a poor system design, let's say for now that when an order is canceled by a customer, it gets deleted from the source system. To take deletions into account, I'll make a minor modification to the model refresh to ignore deletes:

```
TRUNCATE TABLE orders_current;

INSERT INTO orders_current
  (order_status, order_count)
  WITH o_latest AS
  (
    SELECT
      OrderId,
      MAX(LastUpdated) AS max_updated
    FROM Orders_cdc
    GROUP BY orderid
  )
  SELECT o.OrderStatus,
    Count(*) AS order_count
  FROM Orders_cdc o
  INNER JOIN o_latest
    ON o_latest.OrderId = o_latest.OrderId
      AND o_latest.max_updated = o.LastUpdated
  WHERE o.EventType <> 'delete'
  GROUP BY o.OrderStatus;
```

As you can see, the deleted order is no longer considered:

```
SELECT * FROM orders_current;

order_status | order_count
-------------+-------------
Shipped      |            1
Backordered  |            1
(2 rows)
```

Another common use for CDC-ingested data is making sense of the changes themselves. For example, perhaps an analyst wants to know how long, on average, orders take to go from a Backordered to Shipped status. I'll again use a CTE (two this time!) to find the first date that each order was Backordered and Shipped. I'll then subtract the two to get how many days each order that has been both backordered and shipped was in a status of Backordered. Note that this logic intentionally ignores OrderId 3, which is currently backordered but hasn't yet shipped:

```
CREATE TABLE orders_time_to_ship (
  OrderId int,
  backordered_days interval
);

INSERT INTO orders_time_to_ship
  (OrderId, backordered_days)
WITH o_backordered AS
(
  SELECT
    OrderId,
    MIN(LastUpdated) AS first_backordered
  FROM Orders_cdc
  WHERE OrderStatus = 'Backordered'
  GROUP BY OrderId
),
o_shipped AS
(
  SELECT
    OrderId,
    MIN(LastUpdated) AS first_shipped
  FROM Orders_cdc
  WHERE OrderStatus = 'Shipped'
  GROUP BY OrderId
)
SELECT b.OrderId,
  first_shipped - first_backordered
    AS backordered_days
```

```
FROM o_backordered b
INNER JOIN o_shipped s on s.OrderId = b.OrderId;
```

You can see the backorder times of each order as well as use the AVG() function to answer the original question:

```
SELECT * FROM orders_time_to_ship;

orderid | backordered_days
--------+-----------------
      1 | 8 days 00:00:25
      2 | 8 days 01:15:12
(2 rows)

SELECT AVG(backordered_days)
FROM orders_time_to_ship;

avg
-----------------
8 days 00:37:48.5
(1 row)
```

There are numerous other use cases for data that you have a full change history of, but just like modeling data that's been fully loaded or is append-only, there are some common best practices and considerations.

Like the previous section, there are potential performance gains to be made by taking advantage of the fact that data ingested via CDC is loaded incrementally rather than fully refreshed. However, as noted in that section, there are times when the performance gain is not worth the added complexity of an incremental model refresh instead of a full refresh. In the case of working with CDC data, I find this to be true most times. The additional complexity of dealing with both updates and deletes is often enough to make a full refresh the preferred path.

## CHAPTER 7

Orchestrating Pipelines

Previous chapters have described the building blocks of data pipelines, including data ingestion, data transformation, and the steps in a machine learning pipeline. This chapter covers how to "orchestrate," or tie together, those blocks or steps.

Orchestration ensures that the steps in a pipeline are run in the correct order and that dependencies between steps are managed properly.

When I introduced the challenge of orchestrating pipelines in Chapter 2, I also introduced the concept of *workflow orchestration platforms* (also referred to as *workflow management systems* (WMSs), *orchestration platforms*, or *orchestration frameworks*). In this chapter, I will highlight Apache Airflow, which is one of the most popular such frameworks. Though the bulk of the chapter is dedicated to examples in Airflow, the concepts are transferable to other frameworks as well. In fact, I note some alternatives to Airflow later in the chapter.

Finally, the later sections of this chapter discuss some more advanced concepts in pipeline orchestration, including coordinating multiple pipelines on your data infrastructure.

Directed Acyclic Graphs

Though I introduced DAGs in Chapter 2, it's worth repeating what they are. This chapter talks about how they are designed and implemented in Apache Airflow to orchestrate tasks in a data pipeline.

Pipeline steps (tasks) are always *directed*, meaning they start with a task or multiple tasks and end with a specific task or tasks. This is required to guarantee a path of execution. In other words, it ensures that tasks do not run before all their dependent tasks are completed successfully.

Pipeline graphs must also be *acyclic*, meaning that a task cannot point back to a previously completed task. In other words, it cannot cycle back. If it could, then a pipeline could run endlessly!

You'll recall the following example of a DAG from Chapter 2, which is illustrated in Figure 7-1. This is a DAG that was defined in Apache Airflow.

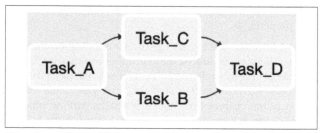

Figure 7-1. A DAG with four tasks. After Task A completes, Task B and Task C run. When they both complete, Task D runs.

Tasks in Airflow can represent anything from the execution of a SQL statement to the execution of a Python script. As you will see in the following sections, Airflow allows you to define, schedule, and execute the tasks in a data pipeline and ensure that they are run in the proper order.

Apache Airflow Setup and Overview

Airflow is an open source project started by Maxime Beauchemin at Airbnb in 2014. It joined the Apache Software Foundation's Incubator program in March 2016. Airflow was built to solve a common challenge faced by data engineering teams: how to build, manage, and monitor workflows (data pipelines in particular) that involve multiple tasks with mutual dependencies.

In the six years since it was first released, Airflow has become one of the most popular workflow management platforms among data teams. Its easy-to-use web interface, advanced command-line utilities, built-in scheduler, and high level of customizability mean that it's a good fit with just about any data infrastructure. Though built in Python, it can execute tasks running on any language or platform. In fact, though most commonly used in managing data pipelines, it's truly a generalized platform for orchestrating any sort of dependent tasks.

NOTE

The code samples and overview in this chapter reference Airflow version 1.x. Airflow 2.0 is on the horizon and promises some major enhancements such as a shiny new Web UI, a new and improved scheduler, a fully featured REST API, and more. Although the specifics of this chapter refer to Airflow 1.x, the concepts will remain true in Airflow 2.0. In addition, the code provided here is intended to work with Airflow 2.0 with little or no modification.

Installing and Configuring

Installing Airflow is thankfully quite simple. You'll need to make use of pip, which was introduced in "Setting Up Your Python Environment" on page 34. As you install and fire up

Airflow for the first time, you'll be introduced to some of its components, such as the Airflow database, web server, and scheduler. I define what each of these are and how they can be further configured in the following sections.

Airflow in a Virtual Environment

Because Airflow is built in Python, you may want to install Airflow into a Python virtual environment (virtualenv). In fact, if you're testing Airflow or running on a machine with other Python projects, I recommend doing so. Refer to "Setting Up Your Python Environment" on page 34 for instructions. If you choose this method, ensure that the name of your virtual environment is created and activated before proceeding.

You can follow the installation instructions from the official Airflow Quick Start Guide (*https://oreil.ly/_fGy8*). This typically takes less than five minutes!

Once you have Airflow installed and the web server running, you can visit *http://localhost:8080* in your browser to view the Airflow web UI. If you'd like to learn more about the various components of Airflow and how they can be configured, the remainder of this section goes into detail on each. If you're ready to build your first Airflow DAG, you can skip ahead to "Building Airflow DAGs" on page 161.

For more advanced deployments of Airflow, I suggest taking a look at the official Airflow documentation (*https://oreil.ly/_VAXS*).

Airflow Database

Airflow uses a database to store all the metadata related to the execution history of each task and DAG as well as your Airflow configuration. By default, Airflow uses a SQLite database. When you ran the `airflow initdb` command during the installation, Airflow created a SQLite database for you. For learning

---

Airflow or even a small-scale project, that's just fine. However, for larger scale needs I suggest using a MySQL or Postgres database. Thankfully, Airflow uses the highly regarded Sql Alchemy library behind the scenes and can easily be reconfigured to use such a database instead of SQLite.

To change which database Airflow uses, you'll need to open the *airflow.cfg* file, which is located in the path you used for AIR FLOW_HOME during installation. In the installation example, that was ~/airflow. In the file, you'll see a line for the sql_alchemy_conn configuration. It will looks something like this:

```
# The SqlAlchemy connection string to the metadata
database.
# SqlAlchemy supports many different database
engine, more information
# their website
sql_alchemy_conn = sqlite:////Users/myuser/airflow/
airflow.db
```

By default the value is set to a connection string for a local SQLite database. In the following example, I'll create and configure a Postgres database and user for Airflow and then configure Airflow to use the new database instead of the default SQLite database.

Note that I assume that you have a Postgres server running and access to run psql (the Postgres interactive terminal) and permission to create databases and users in psql. Any Postgres database will do, but it must be accessible from the machine where Airflow is running. To learn more about installing and configuring a Postgres server, see the official site (*https://www.postgresql.org*). You may also be using a managed Postgres instance on a platform like AWS. That's just fine as long as the machine where Airflow is installed can access it.

First, launch psql on the command line or otherwise open a SQL editor connected to your Postgres server.

Now, create a user for Airflow to use. For simplicity, name it airflow. In addition, set a password for the user:

```
CREATE USER airflow;
ALTER USER airflow WITH PASSWORD 'pass1';
```

Next, create a database for Airflow. I'll call it airflowdb:

```
CREATE DATABASE airflowdb;
```

Finally, grant the new user all privileges on the new database. Airflow will need to both read and write to the database:

```
GRANT ALL PRIVILEGES
  ON DATABASE airflowdb TO airflow;
```

Now you can go back and modify the connection string in the *airflow.cfg* file. I'll assume that your Postgres server is running on the same machine as Airflow, but if not, you'll need to modify the following by replacing localhost with the full path to the host where Postgres is running. Save *airflow.cfg* when you're done:

```
sql_alchemy_conn = postgresql+psycopg2://
airflow:pass1@localhost:5432/airflowdb
```

Since Airflow will need to connect to a Postgres database via Python, you'll also need to install the psycopg2 library:

```
$ pip install psycopg2
```

Finally, go back to the command line to reinitialize the Airflow database in Postgres:

```
$ airflow initdb
```

Going forward, you can find all of the Airflow metadata in the airflowdb database on the Postgres server. There's a wealth of information there, including task history, that can be queried. You can query it directly from the Postrgres database or right in the Airflow web UI, as described in the next section. Having the data queryable via SQL opens up a world of reporting and analysis opportunities. There's no better way to analyze the performance of your pipelines, and you can do it with the data that

---

Airflow collections by default! In Chapter 10 of this book, I discuss using this and other data to measure and monitor the performance of your data pipelines.

Web Server and UI

When you started the web server after installation by running the `airflow webserver -p 8080` command, you may have taken a sneak peek at what it had in store. If not, open a web browser and navigate to *http://localhost:8080*. If you're working with a fresh install of Airflow, you'll see something like Figure 7-2.

Figure 7-2. The Airflow web UI.

The home page of the Web UI shows a list of DAGs. As you can see, Airflow comes with some sample DAGs included. They're a great place to get started if you're new to Airflow. As you create your own DAGs, they'll show up there as well.

There are a number of links and information for each DAG on the page:

- A link to open the properties of the DAG including the path where the source file resides, tags, the description, and so on.

- A toggle to enable and pause the DAG. When enabled, the schedule defined in the fourth column dictates when it runs. When paused, the schedule is ignored, and the DAG can only be run by manual execution.

- The name of the DAG, which, when clicked, brings you to the DAG detail page, as shown in Figure 7-3.

- The schedule that the DAG runs on when not paused. It's shown in crontab format (*https://oreil.ly/btt0G*) and defined in the DAG source file.

- The owner of the DAG. Usually this is airflow but in more complex deployments you may have multiple owners to choose from.

- Recent Tasks, which is a summary of the latest DAG run.

- A timestamp of the last run of the DAG.

- A summary of previous DAG runs.

- A set of links to various DAG configuration and information. You'll also see these links if you click the name of the DAG.

When you click the name of a DAG, you'll be taken to the tree view of the DAG on the DAG detail page, as shown in Figure 7-3. This is the example_python_operator DAG that ships with Airflow. The DAG has five tasks that are all PythonOp erators (you'll learn about operators later in this section). After the print_the_context task completes successfully, five tasks kick off. When they are done, the DAG run is completed.

Figure 7-3. A tree view of a Airflow DAG.

You can also click the Graph View button on the top of the page to see what the DAG looks like as a graph. I find this view to be the most useful. You can see what this particular DAG looks like as a graph in Figure 7-4.

In more complex DAGs with lots of tasks, the graph view can get a little difficult to see on the screen. However, note that you can zoom in and out and scroll around the graph using your mouse.

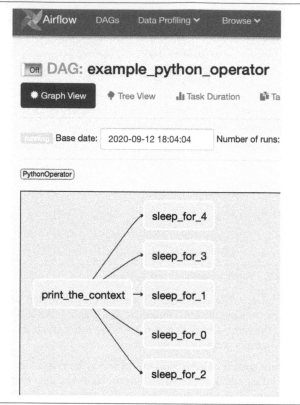

Figure 7-4. A graph view of an Airflow DAG.

There are a number of other options on the screen, many which are self-explanatory. However, I'd like to focus on two more: Code and Trigger DAG.

When you click Code, you'll of course see the code behind the DAG. The first thing you'll notice is that the DAG is defined in a Python script. In this case, the file is called *example_python_operator.py*. You'll learn more about the structure of a DAG source file later in this chapter. For now, it's important to know that it holds the configuration of the DAG, including its schedule, a definition of each task, and the dependencies between each task.

The Trigger DAG button allows you to execute the DAG on-demand. Though Airflow is built to run DAGs on a schedule, during development, during testing, and for off-schedule needs in production, this is the easiest way to run a DAG right away.

Besides managing DAGs, there are a number of other features of the web UI that will come in handy. On the top navigation bar, if you click Data Profiling, you'll see options for Ad Hoc Query, Charts, and Known Events. Here you can query information from the Airflow database if you'd rather not connect to it directly from another tool.

Under Browse, you can find the run history of DAGs and other log files, and under Admin you can find various configuration settings. You can learn more about advanced configuration options in the official Airflow documentation (*https://oreil.ly/OuUS_*).

Scheduler

The Airflow Scheduler is a service that you kicked off when you ran the `airflow scheduler` command earlier in this chapter. When running, the scheduler is constantly monitoring DAGs and tasks and running any that have been scheduled to run or have had their dependencies met (in the case of tasks in a DAG).

The scheduler uses the executor that is defined in the [core] section of the *airflow.cfg* file to run tasks. You can learn about executors in the following section.

Executors

Executors are what Airflow uses to run tasks that the Scheduler determines are ready to run. There are number of different types of executors that Airflow supports. By default, the Sequen tialExecutor is used. You can change the type of executor in the *airflow.cfg* file. Under the core section of the file, you'll see a executor variable that can be set to any of the executor types listed in this section and in the Airflow documentation. As you can see, the SequentialExecutor is set when Airflow is first installed:

```
[core]
........

# The executor class that airflow should use.
Choices include
# SequentialExecutor, LocalExecutor,
CeleryExecutor, DaskExecutor, KubernetesExecutor
executor = SequentialExecutor
```

Though the default, the SequentialExecutor is not meant for production use cases as it can run only one task at a time. It's fine for testing simple DAGs, but that's about it. However, it's the only executor that is compatible with a SQLite database, so if you haven't configured another database with Airflow, the SequentialExecutor is your only option.

If you plan to use Airflow at any sort of scale, I suggest using another executor such as the CeleryExecutor, DaskExecutor, or KubernetesExecutor. Your choice in part should depend on what infrastructure you're most comfortable with. For example, to use the CeleryExecutor, you'll need to set up a Celery broker using RabbitMQ, Amazon SQL, or Redis.

Configuring the infrastructure required by each executor is out of the scope of this book, but the samples in this section will run even on the SequentialExecutor. You can learn more about Airflow executors in their documentation (*https://oreil.ly/YOplY*).

Operators

Recall that each of the nodes in a DAG is a task. In Airflow, each task implements an *operator*. Operators are what actually execute scripts, commands, and other operations. There a number of operators. Here are the most common:

- `BashOperator`
- `PythonOperator`
- `SimpleHttpOperator`
- `EmailOperator`
- `SlackAPIOperator`
- `MySqlOperator`, `PostgresOperator`, and other database-specific operators for executing SQL commands
- `Sensor`

As you'll learn in the following section, operators are instantiated and assigned to each task in a DAG.

Building Airflow DAGs

Now that you know how Airflow works, it's time to build a DAG! Though Airflow comes with a collection of sample DAGs, I'm going to follow some samples from earlier in this book and build a DAG that performs the steps of a sample ELT process. Specifically, it will extract data from a database, load it into a data warehouse, and then transform the data into a data model.

A Simple DAG

Before I build the sample ELT DAG, it's important to understand how DAGs are defined in Airflow. A DAG is defined in a Python script, where its structure and task dependencies are written in Python code. Example 7-1 is the definition of a simple DAG with three tasks. It's referred to as a *DAG definition file*. Each task is defined as a `BashOperator`, with the first and third printing out some text and the second sleeping for three seconds. Though it doesn't do anything particularly useful, it's fully functional and representative of the DAG definitions you'll write later.

Example 7-1. simple_dag.py

```python
from datetime import timedelta
from airflow import DAG
from airflow.operators.bash_operator \
    import BashOperator
from airflow.utils.dates import days_ago

dag = DAG(
    'simple_dag',
    description='A simple DAG',
    schedule_interval=timedelta(days=1),
    start_date = days_ago(1),
)

t1 = BashOperator(
    task_id='print_date',
    bash_command='date',
    dag=dag,
)

t2 = BashOperator(
    task_id='sleep',
    depends_on_past=False,
    bash_command='sleep 3',
    dag=dag,
)

t3 = BashOperator(
    task_id='print_end',
    depends_on_past=False,
    bash_command='echo \'end\'',
    dag=dag,
)

t1 >> t2
t2 >> t3
```

Before you move on and run the DAG, I'd like to point out the key features of the DAG definition file. First, like any Python script, necessary modules are imported. Next, the DAG itself is defined and assigned some properties such as a name (`sim ple_dag`), a schedule, a start date, and more. In fact, there are many more properties that I don't define in this simple example that you may need to utilize and can find later in the chapter or in the official Airflow documentation.

Next, I define the three tasks in the DAG. All are of type `BashOp erator`, meaning when executed, they'll run a bash command. Each task is also assigned several properties, including an alphanumeric identifier called `task_id`, as well as the bash command that runs when the task is executed. As you'll see later, each operator type has its own custom properties just as the `BashOperator` has `bash_command`.

The last two lines of the DAG definition define the dependencies between the tasks. The way to read it is that when the task `t1` completes, `t2` runs. When `t2` completes, `t3` runs. When you view the DAG in the Airflow web UI, you'll see this reflected in both the tree and graph view.

To run the DAG, you'll need to save its definition file in the location where Airflow is looking for DAGs. You can find this location (or modify it) in the *airflow.cfg* file:

```
dags_folder = /Users/myuser/airflow/dags
```

Save the DAG definition in a file named *simple_dag.py* and place it in the *dags_folder* location. If you already have the Airflow web UI and Scheduler running, refresh the Airflow web UI, and you should see a DAG named `simple_dag` in the listing. If not, wait a few seconds and try again, or stop and restart the web service.

Next, click the name of the DAG to view it in more detail. You'll be able to see the graph and tree view of the DAG as well as the code that you just wrote. Ready to give it a try? Either on this screen or back on the home page, flip the toggle so that the DAG is set to On, as shown in Figure 7-5.

Figure 7-5. An enabled DAG.

Recall that in the code, the `schedule_interval` property of the DAG is set to `timedelta(days=1)`. That means the DAG is set to run once a day at midnight UTC. You'll see that schedule reflected on both the Airflow home page next to the DAG and on the DAG detail page. Also note that the `start_date` property of the DAG is set to `days_ago(1)`. That means the first run of the DAG is set one day prior to the current day. When the DAG is set to On, the first scheduled run is 0:00:00 UTC on the day prior the current day and thus will execute as soon as the executor has availability.

DAG Start and End Dates

In this example, I set the `start_date` of the DAG to one day prior so that as soon as I enabled it, a run would get scheduled and kick off. It may make more sense to the hard-code a date in the future as well, say, the day when you want the DAG to first run on a production deployment of Airflow. You can also set an `end_date` for a DAG, which I did not. When none is specified, the DAG will be scheduled to run each day in perpetuity.

You can check on the status of a DAG run on the DAG detail page or by navigating to Browse → DAG Runs on the top menu. From there you should see a visual status of the DAG run, as well as each task in the DAG. Figure 7-6 shows a run of the `simple_dag` example where all tasks succeeded. The final status of the DAG is marked as "success" near the top left of the screen.

If you want to run the DAG on-demand, click the Trigger DAG button on the DAG detail page.

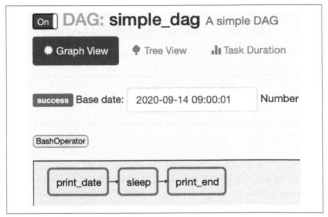

Figure 7-6. A graph view of an Airflow DAG.

An ELT Pipeline DAG

Now that you know how to create a simple DAG, you can build a functional DAG for the extract, load, and transform steps of a data pipeline. This DAG consists of five tasks.

The first two tasks use BashOperators to execute two different Python scripts that each extract data from a Postgres database table and send the results as a CSV file to an S3 bucket. Though I won't re-create the logic for the scripts here, you can find it in "Extracting Data from a PostgreSQL Database" on page 63. In fact, you can use any of the extraction examples from that chapter if you want to extract from a MySQL database, REST API, or MongoDB database.

When each of those tasks completes, a corresponding task to load the data from the S3 bucket into a data warehouse is executed. Once again, each task uses a BashOperator to execute a Python script that contains the logic to load the CSV. You can find the sample code for that in "Loading Data into a Snowflake

Data Warehouse" on page 97 or "Loading Data into a Redshift Warehouse" on page 86, depending on which platform you use.

Options for Executing Python Code

In this example, I utilize the `BashOperator` to execute Python scripts instead of using the `PythonOperator`. Why? In order to execute Python code with the `PythonOperator`, the code must be either written in the DAG definition file or imported into it. While I could have done that in this example, I like to keep a greater separation between my orchestration and the logic of the processes that it executes. For one thing, by doing so I avoid potential issues of incompatible versions of Python libraries between Airflow and any of my own code that I want to execute. In general, I find it easier to maintain logic across a data infrastructure by keeping projects (and Git repos) separated. Orchestration and pipeline process logic is no different.

The final task in the DAG uses a `PostgresOperator` to execute a SQL script (stored in a *.sql* file) on the data warehouse to create a data model. You'll recall this logic from Chapter 6. Together, these five tasks make up a simple pipeline following the ELT pattern first introduced in Chapter 3.

Figure 7-7 shows a graph view of the DAG.

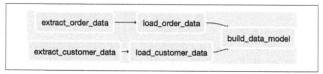

Figure 7-7. Graph view of the sample ELT DAG.

Example 7-2 shows the definition of the DAG. Take a moment to read it, even though I'll walk through it in detail as well. You can save it to the Airflow *dags* folder, but don't enable it just yet.

Example 7-2. elt_pipeline_sample.py

```python
from datetime import timedelta
from airflow import DAG
from airflow.operators.bash_operator \
  import BashOperator
from airflow.operators.postgres_operator \
  import PostgresOperator
from airflow.utils.dates import days_ago

dag = DAG(
    'elt_pipeline_sample',
    description='A sample ELT pipeline',
    schedule_interval=timedelta(days=1),
    start_date = days_ago(1),
)

extract_orders_task = BashOperator(
    task_id='extract_order_data',
    bash_command='python /p/extract_orders.py',
    dag=dag,
)

extract_customers_task = BashOperator(
    task_id='extract_customer_data',
    bash_command='python /p/extract_customers.py',
    dag=dag,
)

load_orders_task = BashOperator(
    task_id='load_order_data',
    bash_command='python /p/load_orders.py',
    dag=dag,
)

load_customers_task = BashOperator(
    task_id='load_customer_data',
    bash_command='python /p/load_customers.py',
    dag=dag,
)
```

```
revenue_model_task = PostgresOperator(
    task_id='build_data_model',
    postgres_conn_id='redshift_dw',
    sql='/sql/order_revenue_model.sql',
    dag=dag,
)

extract_orders_task >> load_orders_task
extract_customers_task >> load_customers_task
load_orders_task >> revenue_model_task
load_customers_task >> revenue_model_task
```

From Example 7-1, you'll recall importing some necessary Python packages and creating a DAG object. This time around, there's one more package to import to make use of the Postgre sOperator in the final task of the DAG. This DAG, like the previous sample, is scheduled to run once a day at midnight, starting the previous day.

The final task utilizes a PostgresOperator to execute a SQL script stored in a directory on the same machine as Airflow on the data warehouse. The contents of the SQL script will look something like the data model transforms from Chapter 6. For example, given the DAG is extracting and loading an Orders table and a Customers table, I'll use the following sample from Chapter 6. You can of course use any SQL query to match the data you're working with.

```
CREATE TABLE IF NOT EXISTS order_summary_daily (
order_date date,
order_country varchar(10),
total_revenue numeric,
order_count int
);

INSERT INTO order_summary_daily
  (order_date, order_country,
  total_revenue, order_count)
SELECT
  o.OrderDate AS order_date,
```

```
      c.CustomerCountry AS order_country,
      SUM(o.OrderTotal) AS total_revenue,
      COUNT(o.OrderId) AS order_count
  FROM Orders o
  INNER JOIN Customers c
    ON c.CustomerId = o.CustomerId
  GROUP BY
    o.OrderDate, c.CustomerCountry;
```

Before you enable the DAG, there's one more step. That is to set the connection to use for the PostgresOperator. As you can see in the DAG definition, there is a parameter called post gres_conn_id with a value of redshift_dw. You'll need to define the redshift_dw connection in the Airflow web UI so that the PostgresOperator can execute the script.

To do so, follow these steps:

1. Open the Airflow web UI and select Admin → Connections from the top navigation bar.

2. Click the Create tab.

3. Set Conn ID to *redshift_dw* (or whatever ID you want to use in your DAG definition file).

4. Select Postgres for Conn Type.

5. Set the connection information for your database.

6. Click Save.

Note that Amazon Redshift is compatible with Postgres connections, which I why I chose that Conn Type. You'll find connections for Snowflake and dozens of other databases and platforms such as Spark.

Now, you're ready to enable the DAG. You can go back to the home page or view the DAG detail page and click the toggle to set the DAG to On. Because the schedule of the DAG is daily at midnight starting the previous day, a run will be scheduled immediately, and the DAG will execute. You can check on the status of a DAG run on the DAG detail page, or by navigating to Browse → DAG Runs on the top menu. As always, you can trigger a one-time run of the DAG using the Trigger DAG button on the DAG detail page.

Though this example is a bit simplified, it pieces together the steps of an ELT pipeline. In a more complex pipeline, you will find many more tasks. In addition to more data extracts and loads, there will likely be many data models, some of which are dependent on each other. Airflow makes it easy to ensure they are executed in the proper order. On most production deployments of Airflow you'll find many DAGs for pipelines that may have some dependency on each other, or some external system or process. See "Advanced Orchestration Configurations" on page 171 for some tips on managing such challenges.

Additional Pipeline Tasks

In addition to the functional tasks in the sample ELT pipeline in the previous section, production-quality pipelines require other tasks, such as sending notifications to a Slack channel when a pipeline completes or fails, running data validation checks at various points in a pipeline, and more. Thankfully, all of these tasks can be handled by an Airflow DAG.

Alerts and Notifications

Although the Airflow web UI is a great place to view the status of DAG runs, it's often better to receive an email when DAG fails (or even when it succeeds). There are a number of options for sending notifications. For example, if you want to get an email when a DAG fails, you can add the following parameters when you instantiate the DAG object in the definition file. You can also add these to tasks instead of the DAG if you only want to be notified for particular tasks:

```
'email': ['me@example.com'],
'email_on_failure': True,
```

Before Airflow can send you email, you'll need to provide the details of your SMTP server in the [smtp] section of *airflow.cfg*.

You can also use the `EmailOperator` in a task to send an email at any point in a DAG:

```
email_task = EmailOperator(
        task_id='send_email',
        to="me@example.com",
        subject="Airflow Test Email",
        html_content='some test content',
    )
```

In addition to the `EmailOperator`, there are both official and community-supported operators for sending messages to Slack, Microsoft Teams, and other platforms. Of course, you can always create your own Python script to send a message to the platform of your choice and execute it using a `BashOperator`.

Data Validation Checks

Chapter 8 discusses data validation and testing pipelines in more detail, but adding task to your Airflow DAGs to run validation on data is a good practice. As you'll learn in that chapter, data validation may be implemented in a SQL or Python script or by calling some other external application. By now you know that Airflow can handle them all!

Advanced Orchestration Configurations

The previous section introduced a simple DAG that runs a full, end-to-end data pipeline that follows the ELT pattern. This section introduces a few challenges you may face when building more complex pipelines or find the need to coordinate multiple pipelines with shared dependencies or different schedules.

Coupled Versus Uncoupled Pipeline Tasks

Though the examples so far may make it seem that all steps (tasks) in a data pipeline are linked together cleanly, that is not always the case. Take a streaming data ingestion. For example, say Kafka is used to stream data to an S3 bucket where it is continuously loaded into a Snowflake data warehouse using Snowpipe (see Chapters 4 and 5).

In this case, data is continuously flowing into the data warehouse, but the step to transform the data will still be scheduled to run at a set interval such as every 30 minutes. Unlike the DAG in Example 7-2, specific runs of the data ingestions are not direct dependencies of the task to transform the data into a data model. In such a situation, the tasks are said to be *uncoupled* as opposed to the *coupled* tasks in a DAG.

Given this reality, data engineers must be thoughtful in how they orchestrate pipelines. Though there are no hard rules, it's necessary to make consistent and resilient decisions throughout pipelines in order to manage decoupled tasks. In the example of streaming data ingestions and a scheduled transform step, the transform logic must take into account that data from two different sources (say the Orders and Customers tables) might be in slightly different states of refresh. The transform logic must take into account cases where there is an Order record without a corresponding Customer record, for example.

When to Split Up DAGs

A key decision point in designing pipelines is determining what tasks belong together in a DAG. Though it's possible to create a DAG with all the extract, load, transform, validation, and alerting tasks on your data infrastructure, it's going to get overly complex pretty quickly.

Three factors go into determining when tasks should be broken out into multiple DAGs and when they should remain in a single DAG:

When the tasks need to run on different schedules, break into multiple DAGS

If you have some that only need to run daily, and some that run every 30 minutes, you should likely split them into two DAGs. Otherwise, you'll waste time and resources to run some tasks 47 extra times per day! In a world where compute costs are frequently based on actual usage, that's a big deal.

When a pipeline is truly independent, keep it separate

If the tasks in the pipeline only relate to each other, then keep them in a single DAG. Going back to Example 7-2, if the Orders and Customer table ingestions are only used by the data model in that DAG and no other tasks rely on the data model, then it makes sense for the DAG to remain on its own.

When a DAG becomes too complex, determine whether you can break it out logically

Though this is a bit subjective, if you find yourself looking at a graph view of a DAG with hundreds of tasks and a spider web of dependency arrows, it's time to consider how to break up the DAG. Otherwise, you may find it hard to maintain in the future.

Though it may seem like a headache to deal with multiple DAGs that may share dependencies (for example, a data ingestion), it's often necessary. In the next section, I discuss how to implement cross-DAG dependencies in Airflow.

Coordinating Multiple DAGs with Sensors

Given the need for shared dependencies between DAGs, Airflow tasks can implement a special type of operator called a Sensor. An Airflow Sensor is designed to check the status of some external task or process and then continue execution of downstream dependencies in its DAG when the check criteria has been met.

If you find the need to coordinate two different Airflow DAGs, you can use a ExternalTaskSensor to check the status of a task in another DAG or the status of another DAG in full. Example 7-3 defines a DAG with two tasks. The first uses an ExternalTaskSensor to check the status of the elt_pipe line_sample DAG from an earlier section of this chapter. When that DAG completes, then the Sensor is marked as "success" and the second task ("task1") is executed.

Example 7-3. sensor_test.py

```python
from datetime import datetime
from airflow import DAG
from airflow.operators.dummy_operator \
  import DummyOperator
from airflow.sensors.external_task_sensor \
  import ExternalTaskSensor
from datetime import timedelta
from airflow.utils.dates import days_ago

dag = DAG(
        'sensor_test',
        description='DAG with a sensor',
        schedule_interval=timedelta(days=1),
        start_date = days_ago(1))

sensor1 = ExternalTaskSensor(
            task_id='dag_sensor',
            external_dag_id = 'elt_pipeline_sample',
            external_task_id = None,
            dag=dag,
            mode = 'reschedule',
            timeout = 2500)

task1 = DummyOperator(
            task_id='dummy_task',
            retries=1,
            dag=dag)

sensor1 >> task1
```

Figure 7-8 shows the graph view of the DAG.

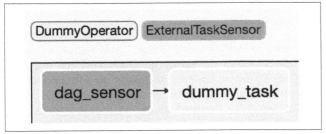

Figure 7-8. Graph view of the sample ELT DAG.

When enabled, this DAG will first kick off the dag_sensor task.
Note its properties:

- The external_dag_id is set to the ID of the DAG that the
  Sensor will monitor. In this case, it's the elt_pipeline_sam
  ple DAG.

- The external_task_id property is set to None in this case,
  which means that the Sensor is waiting on the entire
  elt_pipeline_sample DAG to complete successfully. If you
  were to instead set this to a particular task_id in the
  elt_pipeline_sample DAG, as soon as that task_id completed successfully, sensor1 would complete and kick off
  dummy_task.

- The mode property is set to reschedule. By default, sensors
  run with the poke mode. In that mode, the sensor blocks a
  worker slot while "poking" to check on the external task.
  Depending on what kind of executor you're using, and
  how many tasks are being run, this is not ideal. In resched
  ule mode, the worker slot is released by rescheduling the
  task and thus opening up a worker slot until it is set to run
  again.

- The timeout parameter is set to the number of seconds the
  ExternalTaskSensor will continue to check its external
  dependency before it times out. It's good practice to set a

reasonable timeout here; otherwise, the DAG will continue to run in perpetuity.

One thing to keep in mind is that DAGs run on a specific schedule, and thus the Sensor needs to check for a specific DAG run. By default, the ExternalTaskSensor will check for the run of the external_dag_id with the current schedule of the DAG it belongs to. Because both the elt_pipeline_sample and sensor_test DAGs run once per day at midnight, it's fine to go with the default. However, if the two DAGs run on different schedules, then it's best to specify which run of the elt_pipe line_sample the Sensor should check on. You can do this using either the execution_delta or execution_date_fn parameter of the ExternalTaskSensor. The execution_date_fn parameter defines a specific datetime of a DAG run, and I find it to be less useful than execution_delta.

The execution_delta parameter can be used to look back at a specific run of a DAG. For example, to look at the most recent run of a DAG that is scheduled for every 30 minutes, you would create a task that is defined like this:

```
sen1 = ExternalTaskSensor(
           task_id='dag_sensor',
           external_dag_id = 'elt_pipeline_sample',
           external_task_id = None,
           dag=dag,
           mode = 'reschedule',
           timeout = 2500,
           execution_delta=timedelta(minutes=30))
```

Managed Airflow Options

Though installing a simple Airflow instance is pretty straightforward, it becomes much more of challenge at production scale. Dealing with more complex executors to handle greater parallelization of tasks, keeping your instance up-to-date, and scaling underlying resources are jobs that not every data engineer has the time to take on.

Like many other open source tools, there are several fully managed solutions for Airflow. Two of the most well known are Cloud Composer (*https://oreil.ly/ratu0*) on Google Cloud and Astronomer (*https://oreil.ly/yM7d8*). Though you'll incur a monthly fee that will far exceed running Airflow on a server of your own, the administration aspects of Airflow are taken care of.

Similar to some of the build versus buy decisions throughout this book, hosting Airflow on your own versus choosing a managed solution depends on your particular situation:

- Do you have a systems operations team that can help you self-host?

- Do you have the budget to spend on a managed service?

- How many DAGs and tasks make up your pipelines? Are you running at a high enough scale to require more complex Airflow executors?

- What are your security and privacy requirements? Are you comfortable allowing an external service to connect to your internal data and systems?

Other Orchestration Frameworks

Though this chapter is focused on Airflow, it's by no means the only game in town. There are some other great orchestration frameworks such as Luigi (*https://oreil.ly/QU2FZ*) and Dagster (*https://docs.dagster.io*). Kubeflow Pipelines (*https://www.kubeflow.org*), which is geared toward machine learning pipeline orchestration, is also well supported and popular in the ML community.

When it comes to orchestration of the transform step for data models, dbt (*https://www.getdbt.com*) by Fishtown Analytics is an excellent option. Like Airflow, it's an open source product built in Python, so you can run it on your own at no cost or choose to pay for a managed version, called *dbt Cloud*. Some organizations choose to use Airflow or another general orchestrator for their data ingestions and to run things like Spark jobs, but then use dbt for transforming their data models. In such a case, dbt job runs are triggered by a task in an Airflow DAG, with dbt handling the dependencies between data models on its own. Some examples of using dbt are included in Chapter 9.

Data Validation in Pipelines

Even in the best designed data pipeline, something is bound to go wrong. Many issues can be avoided, or at least mitigated, with good design of processes, orchestration, and infrastructure. To ensure the quality of and validity of the data itself, however, you'll need to invest in data validation. It's best to assume that untested data is not safe to use in analytics. This chapter discusses the principles of data validation throughout the steps of an ELT pipeline.

Validate Early, Validate Often

Though well intentioned, some data teams leave data validation to the end of a pipeline and implement some kind of validation during transformation or even after all transformations are complete. In this design, they are working with the idea that the data analysts (who typically own the transform logic) are best suited to make sense of the data and determine if there are any quality issues.

In such a design, the data engineers focus on moving data from one system to another, orchestrating pipelines, and maintaining the data infrastructure. Although that's the role of a data engineer, there's one thing missing: by ignoring the content of the data flowing through each step in the pipeline, they are putting trust in the owners of the source systems they ingest from, their own ingestion processes, and the analysts who transform the data. As efficient as such separation of responsibilities sounds, it's likely to end with low data quality and an inefficient debugging process when quality issues are uncovered.

Finding a data quality issue at the end of a pipeline and having to trace it back to the beginning is a worst-case scenario. By validating at each step in a pipeline, you are more likely to find the root cause in the current step rather than a previous one.

Though data engineers can't be expected to have enough context to perform validation for every dataset, they can take the lead by writing noncontextual validation checks as well as providing the infrastructure and templates to enable those team members and stakeholders closer to each step in the pipeline to perform more specific validation.

Source System Data Quality

Given the large number of source systems that are ingested into a typical data warehouse, it's likely that invalid data will make its way into the warehouse during data ingestion at some point. Though it may seem that invalid data of some sort would be found by the source system owner before it could be ingested, it's often not the case for several reasons:

Invalid data may not impact the functioning of the source system itself

The logic of the source system application may work around issues such as duplicate/ambiguous records in a table by deduplicating at the application layer, or fill in NULL date values with a default in the application itself.

The source system may function just fine when records are orphaned

For example, a Customer record might be deleted, but the Order records related to the customer may remain. Though the application might just ignore such Order records, this situation will certainly have an impact on the analysis of the data.

A bug that has not yet been found or fixed may actually exist in the source system

I've encountered multiple instances in my career where a critical issue in a source system was identified by the data team!

NOTE

Regardless of the reason, the bottom line is that a data engineer should never assume that the data they are ingesting is free of quality issues, even if the resulting data loaded into the warehouse perfectly matches its source.

Data Ingestion Risks

In addition to quality issues in the source system, there's the possibility of the data ingestion process itself resulting in a data quality problem. Here are some common examples:

A system outage or timeout in the extract or load step of an ingestion

Though at times such a situation will throw a hard error and halt the pipeline, in others a "silent" failure will result in a partially extracted or loaded dataset.

A logical error in an incremental ingestion

Recall from Chapters 4 and 5 the pattern for an incremental extract. The timestamp of the most recent record from a table in the data warehouse is read, and any records with a more recent timestamp in the source system are then extracted so they an be loaded into the warehouse. A logical error as simple as using a "greater than or equals" operator rather than a "greater than" in a SQL statement can result in duplicate records being ingested. There are numerous other possibilities such as inconsistencies in time zones across systems.

Parsing issues in an extracted file

As you'll recall from Chapters 4 and 5, it's typical for data to be extracted from a source system, stored in a flat file such as a CSV, and then loaded from that file into a data warehouse. When data is translated from a source system into a flat file, there are times when it includes special characters or other character encoding that is unexpected. Depending on how the data engineer and the data warehouse loading mechanism handle such cases, it's possible for records to be discarded or the data contained in the newly loaded records to be malformed.

NOTE

Like the assumption that source systems will present valid data, the assumption that a data ingestion "simply" extracts and loads data is a poor one.

Enabling Data Analyst Validation

When it comes to validating the data that's been loaded into a data warehouse and the data that's been transformed into data models, a data analyst is usually the best equipped to own validation. They are the ones who understand the business context of the raw data as well as in each data model (see Chapter 6). However, it's up to data engineers to provide analysts with the tools they need to define and execute data validation throughout a data pipeline. Of course, for less contextual validations such as row counts and duplicate records, data engineers should take part in validation early in the pipeline.

The next section introduces a simplified framework that can be used by analysts and data engineers to implement data validation checks in a pipeline. The final section notes a few open

---

source and commercial frameworks that can be used for the same purpose. Whatever tool you choose, it's important to empower engineers and analysts with a reliable method of writing and executing validation tests while introducing as little friction as possible. Though everyone on a data team tends to agree that valid data is important, if the bar to implement validation is high, you'll find that it will take a backseat to new development and other priorities.

A Simple Validation Framework

In this section, I define a fully functional data validation framework written in Python and designed to execute SQL-based data validation checks. Like other samples in this book, it's highly simplified and lacks many features you'd expect in a production environment. In other words, it's not intended to handle all of your data validation needs. However, my goal is for it to introduce the key concepts of such a framework while also sharing something that can be extended and improved to fit your infrastructure.

This simple version of the framework supports limited capabilities as far as what kind of outcomes can be checked in a validation test and how tests can be executed in bulk, but not much more. I note some possible additions to extend the framework later in this section if you want to use it as a starting point. Even if you choose to use an off-the-shelf framework, I believe there is value in understanding the concepts involved in this highly simplified approach.

Validator Framework Code

The general concept of this framework is a Python script that executes a pair of SQL scripts and compares the two based on a comparison operator. The combination of each script and the outcome is considered a *validation test*, and the test is said to pass or fail depending on how the result of the executed scripts compares to the expected outcome. For example, one script might count the number of rows in a table for a given day, the second counts the number of rows from the previous day, and a comparison operator of >= checks to see if the current day has more rows than the previous did. If so, it passes; if not, it fails.

Note that one of the SQL scripts can also return a static value such as an integer. As you can see in the examples in "Validation Test Examples" on page 198, that approach is used to check for duplicated rows in a table. Though simple, this framework can handle a wide range of validation logic.

Using command-line arguments, you can tell the validator to execute a specific pair of scripts as well as the operator to use for comparison. It then executes and returns a pass/fail code. The return value can be used to trigger various actions in an Airflow DAG, as shown later in this section, or consumed by any other process that executes the validator.

Example 8-1 shows the code for the validator. This version is set to execute tests against an Amazon Redshift data warehouse using the psycopg2 Python library. It also uses the same *pipeline.conf* configuration file from Chapters 4 and 5 to access the credentials to the warehouse. You can easily modify this script to access a Snowflake data warehouse per the samples in Chapter 5, or another data warehouse of your choice. The only difference will be the library you use to connect and execute queries. You'll also need to make sure that your Python environment is set up properly and a virtual environment is activated. See "Setting Up Your Python Environment" on page 34 for more information.

Example 8-1. validator.py

```
import sys
import psycopg2
import configparser

def connect_to_warehouse():
    # get db connection parameters from the conf file
```

```
    parser = configparser.ConfigParser()
    parser.read("pipeline.conf")
    dbname = parser.get("aws_creds", "database")
    user = parser.get("aws_creds", "username")
    password = parser.get("aws_creds", "password")
    host = parser.get("aws_creds", "host")
    port = parser.get("aws_creds", "port")

    rs_conn = psycopg2.connect(
        "dbname=" + dbname
        + " user=" + user
        + " password=" + password
        + " host=" + host
        + " port=" + port)

    return rs_conn

# execute a test made of up two scripts
# and a comparison operator
# Returns true/false for test pass/fail
def execute_test(
        db_conn,
        script_1,
        script_2,
        comp_operator):

    # execute the 1st script and store the result
    cursor = db_conn.cursor()
    sql_file = open(script_1, 'r')
    cursor.execute(sql_file.read())

    record = cursor.fetchone()
    result_1 = record[0]
    db_conn.commit()
    cursor.close()

    # execute the 2nd script and store the result
    cursor = db_conn.cursor()
    sql_file = open(script_2, 'r')
    cursor.execute(sql_file.read())
```

```python
        record = cursor.fetchone()
        result_2 = record[0]
        db_conn.commit()
        cursor.close()

        print("result 1 = " + str(result_1))
        print("result 2 = " + str(result_2))

        # compare values based on the comp_operator
        if comp_operator == "equals":
            return result_1 == result_2
        elif comp_operator == "greater_equals":
            return result_1 >= result_2
        elif comp_operator == "greater":
            return result_1 > result_2
        elif comp_operator == "less_equals":
            return result_1 <= result_2
        elif comp_operator == "less":
            return result_1 < result_2
        elif comp_operator == "not_equal":
            return result_1 != result_2

        # if we made it here, something went wrong
        return False

if __name__ == "__main__":

    if len(sys.argv) == 2 and sys.argv[1] == "-h":
        print("Usage: python validator.py"
            + "script1.sql script2.sql "
            + "comparison_operator")
        print("Valid comparison_operator values:")
        print("equals")
        print("greater_equals")
        print("greater")
        print("less_equals")
        print("less")
        print("not_equal")
```

```
      exit(0)

if len(sys.argv) != 4:
    print("Usage: python validator.py"
      + "script1.sql script2.sql "
      + "comparison_operator")
    exit(-1)

script_1 = sys.argv[1]
script_2 = sys.argv[2]
comp_operator = sys.argv[3]

# connect to the data warehouse
db_conn = connect_to_warehouse()

# execute the validation test
test_result = execute_test(
                db_conn,
                script_1,
                script_2,
                comp_operator)


print("Result of test: " + str(test_result))

if test_result == True:
    exit(0)
else:
    exit(-1)
```

The following subsections describe the structure of the validation tests that this framework is designed to run and how to run a test from the command line as well as an Airflow DAG. In the next section, I'll share some sample validation tests based on common types of tests.

Structure of a Validation Test

As briefly described in the previous subsection, a validation test in this framework consists of three things:

- A SQL file that runs a script that results in a single numeric value

- A second SQL file that runs a script that results in a single numeric value

- A "comparison operator" that is used to compare the two values returned from the SQL scripts

Let's look at a simple example that checks to make sure that two tables have the same number of rows. In Example 8-2, the SQL script counts the number of rows in a table named Orders, while in Example 8-3, the SQL script gets the same count from another table named Orders_Full.

Example 8-2. order_count.sql

```
SELECT COUNT(*)
FROM Orders;
```

Example 8-3. order_full_count.sql

```
SELECT COUNT(*)
FROM Orders_Full;
```

You can use the following SQL to create and populate the Orders and Orders_Full tables used in examples throughout this chapter:

```
CREATE TABLE Orders (
  OrderId int,
  OrderStatus varchar(30),
  OrderDate timestamp,
  CustomerId int,
  OrderTotal numeric
);

INSERT INTO Orders
  VALUES(1,'Shipped','2020-06-09',100,50.05);
INSERT INTO Orders
```

```
    VALUES(2,'Shipped','2020-07-11',101,57.45);
INSERT INTO Orders
    VALUES(3,'Shipped','2020-07-12',102,135.99);
INSERT INTO Orders
    VALUES(4,'Shipped','2020-07-12',100,43.00);

CREATE TABLE Orders_Full (
    OrderId int,
    OrderStatus varchar(30),
    OrderDate timestamp,
    CustomerId int,
    OrderTotal numeric
);

INSERT INTO Orders_Full
VALUES(1,'Shipped','2020-06-09',100,50.05);
INSERT INTO Orders_Full
VALUES(2,'Shipped','2020-07-11',101,57.45);
INSERT INTO Orders_Full
VALUES(3,'Shipped','2020-07-12',102,135.99);
INSERT INTO Orders_Full
VALUES(4,'Shipped','2020-07-12',100,43.00);
```

The last piece of a validation test is the comparison operator to be used to compare the two values. In the code sample from Example 8-1, you can see the options available for comparison operators, but here they are with their associated logical symbols in parentheses for reference:

- equals
- greater_equals
- greater
- less_equals
- less
- not_equal

Next we'll look at how to run a test and make sense of the result.

Running a Validation Test

Using the example of the validation test from the previous subsection, the test can be executed on the command line as follows:

```
$ python validator.py order_count.sql
order_full_count.sql equals
```

If the row counts of both the Orders and Orders_Full tables are the same, the output will look like this:

```
result 1 = 15368
result 2 = 15368
Result of test: True
```

What you don't see on the command line is the *Exit Status Code*, which in this case is 0 but will be -1 in the case of a test failure. You can consume this value programmatically, however. The next section shows how to do so in an Airflow DAG. You may also want to consider doing something like sending a Slack message or email when a test fails. I'll discuss some options for doing that later in "Extending the Framework" on page 193.

Usage in an Airflow DAG

As you learned in Chapter 7, an Airflow task can execute a Python script using a BashOperator. Consider the elt_pipe line_sample DAG from Example 7-2. After the Orders table is ingested (after both the extract and load tasks), I will add another task to run the validation test example I just shared to check the row count of the Orders table against some fictional table named Orders_Full. For the sake of this example, assume that for some reason we want to make sure that the row count in Orders is the same as Orders_Full, and if it's not, to fail the task and stop further execution of downstream tasks in the DAG.

First, add the following task to the elt_pipeline_sample.py DAG definition:

```
check_order_rowcount_task = BashOperator(
    task_id='check_order_rowcount',
    bash_command='set -e; python validator.py' +
    'order_count.sql order_full_count.sql equals',
    dag=dag,
)
```

Next, redefine the dependency order of the DAG in the same file to the following code. This ensures that after the load_orders_task, the validation task runs, followed by the revenue_model_task once both the validation is completed (and passed) and the load_customers_task has completed successfully:

```
extract_orders_task >> load_orders_task
extract_customers_task >> load_customers_task
load_orders_task >> check_order_rowcount_task
check_order_rowcount_task >> revenue_model_task
load_customers_task >> revenue_model_task
```

Figure 8-1 shows the updated graph view of the DAG.

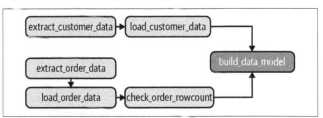

Figure 8-1. Graph view of the sample ELT DAG with a validation test included.

When check_order_rowcount_task is executed, the following Bash command is run per the task definition:

```
set -e; python validator.py order_count.sql
order_full_count.sql equals
```

You'll recognize the execution of the validator with the command-line arguments from earlier in this section. What's new is the set -e; prior to the rest of the command. This tells

Bash to stop execution of the script on an error, which is defined by a nonzero exit status code. As you'll recall, if the validation test fails, it returns an exit status of -1. If that happens, the Airflow task will fail, and no downstream tasks will execute (revenue_model_task in this case).

It's not always necessary to halt the further execution of a DAG when a validation tests fails. In that case, you shouldn't include the set -e portion of the Bash command set on the Airflow task or modify the validator to handle warnings and hard errors differently. Next, I'll discuss when to do so and when to simply send some kind of notification instead.

When to Halt a Pipeline, When to Warn and Continue

There are times, such as in the previous example, when halting a pipeline is necessary when a data validation tests fails. In that example, if the record count in the Orders table is incorrect, perhaps by refreshing the data model in the final task, business users will see incorrect sales figures. If that's important to avoid, then halting the DAG so that the issue can be addressed is the right approach. When that's done, the data model still has data in it from the previous successful run of the DAG. In general, stale data is better than incorrect data!

However, there are other times when the failure of a validation test is less critical and more informational. For example, perhaps the number of orders in the table increased by 3% since the previous run a day ago, while the average daily increase over the previous 30 days was 1%. You may catch such an increase with a basic statistical test as I show in the next section. Is it an issue worth halting for? The answer is that it depends on your circumstances and appetite for risk, but you can rely on multiple tests to get at that answer.

For example, if you were to also run a test to check for duplicate rows in the Orders table and it passed, then you know that the issue isn't some kind of duplication. Perhaps the company just had an incredible day of sales because of a promotion. You can also adjust your test to take into account seasonality. Perhaps it's the holiday season and yesterday was Black Friday. Instead of comparing the growth in records to the past 30 days, you should have compared it to the same period the previous year, with or without an additional factor for growth in the business year over year.

In the end, the decision whether to throw an error and halt a pipeline versus sending an alert to a Slack channel should be based on the context of the business and use case of the data. However, it points to the need for both data engineers and analysts being empowered to contribute validation tests to a pipeline. Although a data engineer may check for a row count discrepancy, they may not have the business context to think of creating a test to check for a seasonality factor in growth of a row count in the Orders table.

What if you want to just warn instead of halt the pipeline? You'll need to make a few modifications either to the DAG in the previous example or to the validation framework itself. Airflow has a number of options for error handling that you can learn about in the official Airflow documentation. In the following section on some possible extensions to the validation framework, I suggest some ways you can handle less critical failures in the framework itself. Either option is fine; it's up to you where you want the logic to live.

Extending the Framework

As I noted earlier in the chapter, the sample data validation framework from Example 8-1 is lacking many features that you'll want to consider for a production deployment. If you decide to use this framework as a starting point rather than considering an open source or commercial option, there are a number of improvements you may want to consider.

A common need in a validation framework is to send a notification to a Slack channel or email when a test fails. I'll provide an example of how to do so for a Slack channel, but there are numerous examples on the Web for sending email and notifications to other messaging services in Python.

First, you'll need to create an *incoming webhook* for the Slack channel you want to send to. An incoming webhook is a URL that is unique to the channel that you can post data to in order for it to show up as a message in that channel. You can follow the instructions in the Slack documentation (*https://oreil.ly/ L4sYZ*) to learn how to create one.

Once you have a webhook, you can add the following function shown in Example 8-4 to validator.py. You can pass information about a validation test to it. The information sent to the webhook is then published in the Slack channel.

Example 8-4. A function to send Slack messages

```
# test_result should be True/False
def send_slack_notification(
  webhook_url,
  script_1,
  script_2,
  comp_operator,
  test_result):
    try:
        if test_result == True:
            message = ("Validation Test Passed!: "
            + script_1 + " / "
            + script_2 + " / "
            + comp_operator)
        else:
            message = ("Validation Test FAILED!: "
            + script_1 + " / "
            + script_2 + " / "
            + comp_operator)

        slack_data = {'text': message}
        response = requests.post(webhook_url,
            data=json.dumps(slack_data),
```

```
    headers={
        'Content-Type': 'application/json'
    })

if response.status_code != 200:
    print(response)
    return False
except Exception as e:
    print("error sending slack notification")
    print(str(e))
    return False
```

Now all you need to do is make a call to the function right before *validation.py* exits. Example 8-5 shows the final lines of the updated script.

Example 8-5. Send a Slack message when a test fails

```
if test_result == True:
    exit(0)
else:
    send_slack_notification(
        webhook_url,
        script_1,
        script_2,
        comp_operator,
        test_result)
    exit(-1)
```

Of course, there is some room for improvement in the formatting of the Slack messages that the function sends, but for now it's enough to get the job done. Note that I included the test_result parameter in the send_slack_notification function. It's set up to handle notifications of passed tests as well as failed ones. Though I don't use it this way in the example, you may want to do so.

As noted in the previous subsection, sometimes a Slack message is sufficient, and the result of a failed test should not result in the pipeline coming to a halt. Though you can make use of the DAG configuration to handle such a case, you can also improve the validation framework by adding another command-line parameter to define severity.

Example 8-6 shows an updated __main__ block of validator.py with handing for severity. When the script is executed with a severity level of halt, then a failed test results in an exit code of -1. When the severity level is set to warn, then a failed test results in an exit code of 0, just as it does when a test passes. In both cases, a failed message leads to a Slack message being sent to your desired channel.

Example 8-6. Add handling for multiple severity levels of test failure

```
if __name__ == "__main__":

    if len(sys.argv) == 2 and sys.argv[1] == "-h":
        print("Usage: python validator.py"
            + "script1.sql script2.sql "
            + "comparison_operator")
        print("Valid comparison_operator values:")
        print("equals")
        print("greater_equals")
        print("greater")
        print("less_equals")
        print("less")
        print("not_equal")

        exit(0)

    if len(sys.argv) != 5:
        print("Usage: python validator.py"
            + "script1.sql script2.sql "
            + "comparison_operator")
        exit(-1)

    script_1 = sys.argv[1]
    script_2 = sys.argv[2]
    comp_operator = sys.argv[3]
```

```python
sev_level = sys.argv[4]

# connect to the data warehouse
db_conn = connect_to_warehouse()

# execute the validation test
test_result = execute_test(
                db_conn,
                script_1,
                script_2,
                comp_operator)


print("Result of test: " + str(test_result))

if test_result == True:
    exit(0)
else:
    send_slack_notification(
      webhook_url,
      script_1,
      script_2,
      comp_operator,
      test_result)
    if sev_level == "halt":
        exit(-1)
    else:
        exit(0)
```

There are countless other ways to extend this framework, two of which follow. I'm sure you'll think of some others as well!

Exception handing through the application

Though I left it out for sake of space in this book, catching and handling exceptions for things like invalid command-line arguments and SQL errors in the test scripts are a must in production.

The ability to run a number of tests with a single execution of
validator.py

Consider storing your tests in a config file and grouping them by table, DAG, or in another way that fits your development pattern. Then you can execute all tests that match a specific point in a pipeline with a single command rather than one for each test you've defined.

Validation Test Examples

The preceding section defined a simple validation framework and the concept behind how it works. As a reminder, a validation test consists of the following:

- A SQL file that runs a script that results in a single numeric value

- A second SQL file that runs a script that results in a single numeric value

- A "comparison operator" that is used to compare the two values returned from the SQL scripts

Assuming you added to enhancements from Examples 8-4, 8-5, and 8-6 to the validator.py code in Example 8-1, you can execute a test on the command line as follows:

```
python validator.py order_count.sql
order_full_count.sql equals warn
```

> ## Severity Level in Examples
>
> Note that I use the warn value for the final command-line parameter (severity_level) shown previously. I'll do so throughout the examples in this section, but you can use the halt value if you want as well. See Example 8-6 for more.

In this section, I'll define some sample tests that I find useful in validating data in a pipeline. These are by no means all of the tests that you'll need to run, but they do cover some common points to get you started and inspire a wider range of tests. Each subsection includes the source for the two SQL files that make up the test as well as the command-line commands and arguments to execute the tests.

Duplicate Records After Ingestion

Checking for duplicate records is a simple, common test. The only thing you'll need to consider is what defines a "duplicate" in the table you're checking. Is it based on a single ID value? An ID as well as a second column? In this example, I'll check to make sure that there are not two records in the Orders table with the same OrderId. To check for duplicates based on additional columns, you can simply add those columns to the SELECT and GROUP BY in the first query.

Note that the second query returns a static value of 0. That's because I expect no duplicates and want to compare the count of duplicates to zero. If they match, the test passes.

Example 8-7. order_dup.sql

```
WITH order_dups AS
(
  SELECT OrderId, Count(*)
  FROM Orders
  GROUP BY OrderId
  HAVING COUNT(*) > 1
)
SELECT COUNT(*)
FROM order_dups;
```

Example 8-8. order_dup_zero.sql

```
SELECT 0;
```

To run the test, use this:

```
python validator.py order_dup.sql
order_dup_zero.sql equals warn
```

Unexpected Change in Row Count After Ingestion

When you expect the number of records from a recent ingestion to be somewhat constant, you can use a statistical check to
see if the latest ingestion loaded more or fewer records than
history would suggest.

In this example, I assume that data is ingested daily and will
look to see if the number of records in the Orders table loaded
most recently (yesterday) is within a range I'm comfortable
with. You can do the same for hourly, weekly, or any other
interval, as long as it's constant.

I'll use a standard deviation calculation and look to see if yesterday's row count is within a 90% confidence level based on
the entire history of the Orders table. In other words, is the
value (number of rows) within a 90% confidence interval in
either direction (can be up to 5% off in either direction) of
what's expected, based on history?

How Far to Look Back

You may want to look back a lesser time period than the entire
history of the table, like a year or two. That decision should be
based on the history of the data. Was there a systematic change
at some point in time? Is history further back than a year accu-
rate? That decision is up to you.

In statistics, this is considered a *two-tailed test* because we are
looking under both sides of a normal distribution curve. You
can use a z-score calculator to determine what score to use for a
two-tailed test with a confidence interval of 90% to determine a
z-score of 1.645. In other words, we're looking for a difference
in either direction, too high or too low, based on a set
threshold.

I'll use that z-score in the test to see if the count of order records from yesterday passes or fails a test. In the validation test, I'll return the absolute value of the z-score for yesterday's row count and then compare it to a z-score of 1.645 in the second SQL script.

Because you need a good deal of sample data in the Orders tables, I provide two versions of the first SQL script in the validation test. The first (Example 8-9) is the "real" code used to go through the Orders table, get row counts by day, and then calculate the z-score for the previous day.

However, you may want to instead use some sample data to experiment with this kind of test. I provide an alternate version to populate a table called orders_by_day and then execute the latter section of Example 8-9 to calculate the z-score for the last day of the sample set (*2020-10-05*). Example 8-11 shows the alternate version.

Example 8-9. order_yesterday_zscore.sql

```
WITH orders_by_day AS (
  SELECT
    CAST(OrderDate AS DATE) AS order_date,
    COUNT(*) AS order_count
  FROM Orders
  GROUP BY CAST(OrderDate AS DATE)
),
order_count_zscore AS (
  SELECT
    order_date,
    order_count,
    (order_count - avg(order_count) over ())
    / (stddev(order_count) over ()) as z_score
  FROM orders_by_day
)
SELECT ABS(z_score) AS twosided_score
FROM order_count_zscore
WHERE
  order_date =
```

```
CAST(current_timestamp AS DATE)
- interval '1 day';
```

Example 8-10 simply returns the value to check against.

Example 8-10. zscore_90_twosided.sql

```
SELECT 1.645;
```

To run the test, use this:

```
python validator.py order_yesterday_zscore.sql
zscore_90_twosided.sql greater_equals warn
```

NOTE

If the Orders table contains a high volume of data, it's worth creating the orders_by_day dataset as a table in a transform task (just as the data model examples in Chapter 6) rather than as a CTE in the validation script. Because the number of orders by day should not change in the past, you can create an incremental data model and append rows for each subsequent day as new data arrives in the Orders table.

Here is the alternative version, with a hard-coded date to check along with the sample data required to run it. With this version, you can adjust the order_count values and run the test to get different z-scores in and out of the desired range:

```
CREATE TABLE orders_by_day
(
  order_date date,
  order_count int
);

INSERT INTO orders_by_day
  VALUES ('2020-09-24', 11);
```

```
    INSERT INTO orders_by_day
      VALUES ('2020-09-25', 9);
    INSERT INTO orders_by_day
      VALUES ('2020-09-26', 14);
    INSERT INTO orders_by_day
      VALUES ('2020-09-27', 21);
    INSERT INTO orders_by_day
      VALUES ('2020-09-28', 15);
    INSERT INTO orders_by_day
      VALUES ('2020-09-29', 9);
    INSERT INTO orders_by_day
      VALUES ('2020-09-30', 20);
    INSERT INTO orders_by_day
      VALUES ('2020-10-01', 18);
    INSERT INTO orders_by_day
      VALUES ('2020-10-02', 14);
    INSERT INTO orders_by_day
      VALUES ('2020-10-03', 26);
    INSERT INTO orders_by_day
      VALUES ('2020-10-04', 11);
```

Example 8-11. order_sample_zscore.sql

```
WITH order_count_zscore AS (
  SELECT
    order_date,
    order_count,
    (order_count - avg(order_count) over ())
    / (stddev(order_count) over ()) as z_score
  FROM orders_by_day
)
SELECT ABS(z_score) AS twosided_score
FROM order_count_zscore
WHERE
  order_date =
    CAST('2020-10-05' AS DATE)
    - interval '1 day';
```

To run the test, use this:

```
python validator.py order_sample_zscore.sql
zscore_90_twosided.sql greater_equals warn
```

Metric Value Fluctuations

As noted earlier in this chapter, validating data at each step of
the pipeline is critical. The previous two examples checked for
the validity of data after ingestion. This example checks to
make sure nothing went wrong after data was modeled in the
transform step of a pipeline.

In the data modeling examples from Chapter 6, multiple source
tables are joined together, and logic that determines how to
aggregate values is implemented. There's no shortage of things
that can go wrong, including invalid join logic that results in
rows being duplicated or dropped. Even if the source data
passed validation earlier in a pipeline, it's always good practice
to run validation on the data models that are built at the end of
a pipeline.

There are three things you can check on:

- Ensuring a metric is within certain lower and upper
  bounds
- Checking row count growth (or reduction) in the data
  model
- Checking to see if there is unexpected fluctuation in the
  value of a particular metric

By now you probably have a good idea of how to implement
such tests, but I will provide one final example for checking
fluctuation in a metric value. The logic is nearly identical to
that of the last section where I shared how to use a two-sided
test to check the change in row count of a given source table.
This time, however, instead of checking a row count value, I'm
looking to see if the total revenue from orders placed on a
given day is out of historical norms.

Like the prior section's example of looking for row count changes, I provide both a "real" example of how to do this on raw data (Example 8-12) as well as one with sample, aggregate data (Example 8-14). To run Example 8-12, you'll need quite a bit of data in the Orders table. This code makes sense for a true implementation. However, you might find Example 8-14 easier to experiment with for the sake of learning.

Example 8-12. revenue_yesterday_zscore.sql

```sql
WITH revenue_by_day AS (
  SELECT
    CAST(OrderDate AS DATE) AS order_date,
    SUM(ordertotal) AS total_revenue
  FROM Orders
  GROUP BY CAST(OrderDate AS DATE)
),
daily_revenue_zscore AS (
  SELECT
    order_date,
    total_revenue,
    (total_revenue - avg(total_revenue) over ())
     / (stddev(total_revenue) over ()) as z_score
  FROM revenue_by_day
)
SELECT ABS(z_score) AS twosided_score
FROM daily_revenue_zscore
WHERE
  order_date =
    CAST(current_timestamp AS DATE)
    - interval '1 day';
```

Example 8-13 simply returns the value to check against.

Example 8-13. zscore_90_twosided.sql

```sql
SELECT 1.645;
```

Use this to run the test:

```
python validator.py revenue_yesterday_zscore.sql
zscore_90_twosided.sql greater_equals warn
```

Here is the sample data for Example 8-14, which as previously noted is a simplified version of Example 8-12 but for your own experimentation:

```
CREATE TABLE revenue_by_day
(
  order_date date,
  total_revenue numeric
);

INSERT INTO revenue_by_day
  VALUES ('2020-09-24', 203.3);
INSERT INTO revenue_by_day
  VALUES ('2020-09-25', 190.99);
INSERT INTO revenue_by_day
  VALUES ('2020-09-26', 156.32);
INSERT INTO revenue_by_day
  VALUES ('2020-09-27', 210.0);
INSERT INTO revenue_by_day
  VALUES ('2020-09-28', 151.3);
INSERT INTO revenue_by_day
  VALUES ('2020-09-29', 568.0);
INSERT INTO revenue_by_day
  VALUES ('2020-09-30', 211.69);
INSERT INTO revenue_by_day
  VALUES ('2020-10-01', 98.99);
INSERT INTO revenue_by_day
  VALUES ('2020-10-02', 145.0);
INSERT INTO revenue_by_day
  VALUES ('2020-10-03', 159.3);
INSERT INTO revenue_by_day
  VALUES ('2020-10-04', 110.23);
```

Example 8-14. revenue_sample_zscore.sql

```
WITH daily_revenue_zscore AS (
  SELECT
    order_date,
```

```
    total_revenue,
    (total_revenue - avg(total_revenue) over ())
    / (stddev(total_revenue) over ()) as z_score
  FROM revenue_by_day
)
SELECT ABS(z_score) AS twosided_score
FROM daily_revenue_zscore
WHERE
  order_date =
    CAST('2020-10-05' AS DATE)
    - interval '1 day';
```

To run the test, use this:

```
python validator.py revenue_sample_zscore.sql
zscore_90_twosided.sql greater_equals warn
```

Of course, you'll want to consider adjusting this test to fit your business case.

Is looking at order revenue by day too "noisy"? Is your order volume low enough that you need to look at weekly or monthly aggregates instead? If so, you can modify Example 8-12 to aggregate by week or month instead of day. Example 8-15 shows a monthly version of the same check. It compares the previous month versus the 11 prior to it.

Note that this example checks the total revenue for the previous month from the current date. This is the type of validation you'd run when you "close" a month, which is usually on the first day of the next month. For example, this is a validation you might run on October 1 to check to make sure that revenue from September is within your expected range based on past history.

Example 8-15. revenue_lastmonth_zscore.sql

```
WITH revenue_by_day AS (
  SELECT
    date_part('month', order_date) AS order_month,
    SUM(ordertotal) AS total_revenue
```

```
  FROM Orders
  WHERE
    order_date > date_trunc('month',current_timestamp
- interval '12 months')
    AND
    order_date < date_trunc('month', current_timestamp)
  GROUP BY date_part('month', order_date)
),
daily_revenue_zscore AS (
  SELECT
    order_month,
    total_revenue,
    (total_revenue - avg(total_revenue) over ())
    / (stddev(total_revenue) over ()) as z_score
  FROM revenue_by_day
)
SELECT ABS(z_score) AS twosided_score
FROM daily_revenue_zscore
WHERE order_month =
date_part('month',date_trunc('month',current_timestamp
- interval '1 months'));
```

There are a number of other variations of such a validation test. What level of date granularity, what date periods you want to compare, and even the z-score are things you'll need to analyze and tweak based on your own data.

Metric Validation Requires Context

Writing validation tests for metric values in a data model can be quite a challenge, and one best left to a data analyst who knows the business context well. Taking into account growth in the business, day of week effects, seasonality, and more is a skill in and of itself and differs for each business and use case. Still, the examples in this section should give you an idea of where to start.

Commercial and Open Source Data Validation Frameworks

Throughout this section, I've used a sample Python-based validation framework. As previously noted, though it's simple, it can easily be extended to become a full-featured, production-ready application for all kinds of data validation needs.

That said, just like data ingestion, data modeling, and data orchestration tools, there is a build-versus-buy decision to make when it comes to what you use for data validation. In fact, previous build-versus-buy decisions often play into what a data team decides to use for data validation at different points in a pipeline.

For instance, some data ingestion tools include features to check for row count changes, unexpected values in columns, and more. Some data transformation frameworks, such as dbt (*https://www.getdbt.com*), include data validation and testing functionally. If you've already invested in such tools, check to see what options are available.

Finally, there are open source frameworks for data validation. The number of such frameworks is vast, and I suggest looking for one that fits your ecosystem. For example, if you're building a machine learning pipeline and use TensorFlow, you might consider TensorFlow Data Validation (*https://oreil.ly/EJHDI*). For more general validation, Yahoo's Validator (*https://oreil.ly/XMdGY*) is an open source option.

## CHAPTER 9

Best Practices for Maintaining Pipelines

Up to this point, this book has been focused on building data pipelines. This chapter discusses how to maintain those pipelines as you encounter increased complexity and deal with the inevitable changes in the systems that your pipelines rely on.

Handling Changes in Source Systems

One of the most common maintenance challenges for data engineers is dealing with the fact that the systems they ingest data from are not static. Developers are always making changes to their software, either adding features, refactoring the codebase, or fixing bugs. When those changes introduce a modification to the schema or meaning of data to be ingested, a pipeline is at risk of failure or inaccuracy.

As discussed throughout this book, the reality of a modern data infrastructure is that data is ingested from a large diversity of sources. As a result, it's difficult to find a one-size-fits-all solution to handling schema and business logic changes in source systems. Nonetheless, there a few best practices I recommend investing in.

Introduce Abstraction

Whenever possible, it's best to introduce a layer of abstraction between the source system and the ingestion process. It's also important for the owner of the source system to either maintain or be aware of the abstraction method.

For example, instead of ingesting data directly from a Postgres database, consider working with the owner of the database to build a REST API that pulls from the database and can be queried for data extraction. Even if the API is simply a passthrough, the fact that it exists in a codebase maintained by the owner of the source system means that the system owner is aware of what data is being extracted and doesn't have to worry about changes to the internal structure of their Postgres application database. If they choose to modify the structure of a database table, they'll need to make a modification to the API but won't need to consider what other code might rely on it.

In addition, if the change to the source system results in the removal of a field that a supported API endpoint includes, then a conscience decision regarding what to do can be made. Perhaps the field is phased out over time or is supported with historical data but is NULL going forward. Either way, there is an awareness of the need to handle the change when an explicit abstraction layer exists.

REST APIs are not the only option for abstraction and at times are not the best fit. Publishing data via a Kafka topic is an excellent way to maintain an agreed-upon schema while leaving the particulars of the source system that publishes an event and the system that subscribes to it (the ingestion) completely separate from each other.

Maintain Data Contracts

If you must ingest data directly from a source system's database or via some method that is not explicitly designed for your extraction, creating and maintaining a data contract is a less technical solution to managing schema and logic changes.

Data Contracts

A *data contract* is a written agreement between the owner of a source system and the team ingesting data from that system for use in a data pipeline. The contract should state what data is being extracted, via what method (full, incremental), how often, as well as who (person, team) are the contacts for both the source system and the ingestion. Data contracts should be stored in a well-known and easy-to-find location such as a Git-Hub repo or internal documentation site. If possible, format data contracts in a standardized form so they can be integrated into the development process or queried programmatically.

A data contract may be written in the form of a text document, but preferably in a standardized configuration file such as in Example 9-1. In this example, a data contract for an ingestion from a table in a Postgres database is stored in JSON form.

Example 9-1. orders_contract.json

```
{
  ingestion_jobid: "orders_postgres",
  source_host: "my_host.com",
  source_db: "ecommerce",
  source_table: "orders",
  ingestion_type: "full",
  ingestion_frequency_minutes: "60",
  source_owner: "dev-team@mycompany.com",
  ingestion_owner: "data-eng@mycompany.com"
};
```

Once you create data contracts, here are some ways you can use them to stay ahead of any source system changes that risk the integrity of your pipelines:

- Build a Git hook that looks for any changes (schema or logic) to a table listed as a `source_table` in a data contract when a PR is submitted or code is committed to a branch. Automatically notify the contributor that the table is used in a data ingestion and who to contact (the `ingestion_owner`) for coordination of the change.

- If the data contract itself is in a Git repo (and it should be!), add a Git hook to check for changes to the contract. For example, if the frequency that the ingestion runs is increased, not only should the data contract be updated, but the source system owner should be consulted to ensure there is not a negative impact on a production system.

- Publish in readable form of all data contracts on the company's centralized documentation site and make them searchable.

- Write and schedule a script to notify source system and ingestion owners of any data contracts that haven't been updated in the past six months (or other frequency) and ask them to review and update if needed.

Whether automated or not, the goal is for changes to the data being ingested or the method of ingestion (say from incremental to full load) to be flagged and communicated ahead of any issues in the pipeline or source system.

Limits of Schema-on-Read

One approach to dealing with changes to the schema of source data is to move from a *schema-on-write* design to *schema-on-read*.

Schema-on-write is the pattern used throughout this book; in particular, in Chapters 4 and 5. When data is extracted from a source, the structure (schema) is defined, and the data is written to the data lake or S3 bucket. Then, when the load step in the ingestion is run, the data is in a predictable form and can be loaded into a defined table structure.

Schema-on-read is a pattern where data is written to a data lake, S3 bucket, or other storage system with no strict schema. For example, an event defining an order placed in a system might be defined as a JSON object, but the properties of that object might change over time as new ones are added or existing ones are removed. In this case, the schema of the data is not known until it's *read*, which is why it's called schema-on-read.

While very efficient for writing data to storage, this pattern adds complexity to the load step and has some major implications in a pipeline. From a technical perspective, reading data stored in this way from an S3 bucket is quite easy. Amazon Athena and other products make querying the raw data as simple as writing a SQL query. However, maintaining the definition of the data is no small task.

First, you'll want to make use of a *data catalog* that integrates with whatever tool you are using to read the schema-flexible data during the load step. A data catalog stores metadata for the data in your data lake and warehouse. It can store both the structure and the definition of datasets. For schema-on-read, it's critical to define and store the structure of data in a catalog for both pragmatic use and human reference. AWS Glue Data Catalog (*https://oreil.ly/BpXT7*) and Apache Atlas (*https://atlas.apache.org*) are popular data catalogs, but there are many more to choose from.

Second, the logic of your load step becomes more complex. You'll need to consider how you'll handle schema changes dynamically. Do you want to dynamically add new columns to a table in your warehouse when new fields are detected during an ingestion? How will you notify data analysts who are modeling the data in the transform step in a pipeline or changes to their source tables?

If you choose to take a schema-on-read approach, you'll want to get serious about *data governance*, which includes not only cataloging your data, but also defining the standards and process around how data is used in an organization. Data governance is a broad topic, and an important one regardless of how you ingest data. However, it's a topic that can't be ignored at a technical level if you do choose a schema-on-read approach.

Scaling Complexity

Building data pipelines when source systems and downstream data models are limited is challenging enough. When those numbers get large, as they do in even relatively small organizations, there are some challenges to scaling pipelines to handle the increased complexity. This section includes some tips and best practices for doing so at various stages of a pipeline.

Standardizing Data Ingestion

When it comes to complexity, the number of systems you ingest from is typically less of an issue than the fact that each system isn't quite the same. That fact often leads to two pipeline maintenance challenges:

- Ingestion jobs must be written to handle a variety of source system types (Postgres, Kafka, and so on). The more source system types you need to ingest from, the larger your codebase and the more to maintain.

- Ingestion jobs for the same source system type cannot be easily standardized. For example, even if you only ingest from REST APIs, if those APIs do not have standardized ways of paging, incrementally accessing data, and other features, data engineers may build "one-off" ingestion jobs that don't reuse code and share logic that can be centrally maintained.

Depending on your organization, you may have little control over the systems you ingest from. Perhaps you must ingest from mostly third-party platforms or the internal systems are built by an engineering team under a different part of the organization hierarchy. Neither is a technical problem, but each should nonetheless be taken into account and addressed as part of a data pipeline strategy. Thankfully, there are also some technical approaches within your control to mitigate the impact on your pipelines.

First, the nontechnical factors. If the systems you're ingesting from are built internally but are not well standardized, creating awareness of the impact on the data organization pipelines can lead to buy-in from system owners.

Especially in larger companies, the software engineers building each system may not be aware that they are building systems that are not quite the same as their counterparts elsewhere in the organization. Thankfully, software engineers typically understand the efficiency and maintainability benefits of standardization. Forging a partnership with the engineering organization requires patience and the right touch, but it's an underrated nontechnical skill for data teams.

If you find yourself needing to ingest from a large number of third-party data sources, then your organization is likely choosing to buy versus build in many instances. Build/buy decisions are complex, and organizations typically weigh many factors when evaluating different vendors and proposals for internally built solutions. One factor that's often either left out or left to later-than-ideal in the process is the impact on reporting and analytics. In such cases, data teams are left with the challenge of ingesting data from a product that wasn't well designed for the task. Do your best to be part of the evaluation process early, and ensure your team has a seat at the table for the final decision. Just like creating awareness for internal system standardization, the importance of working with vendors to determine analytics needs is something that is often not considered unless the data team makes sure their voice is heard.

There are also some technical approaches within your control that you can take to reduce complexity of your ingestion jobs:

Standardize whatever code you can, and reuse
This is a general best practice in software engineering, but is at times passed over in the creating of data ingestion jobs.

Strive for config-driven data ingestions
Are you ingesting from a number of Postgres databases and tables? Don't write a different job for each ingestion, but rather a single job that iterates through config files (or records in a database table!) that defines the tables and schemas you want to ingest.

Consider your own abstractions
If you can't get source system owners to build some standardized abstractions between their systems and your ingestion, consider doing so yourself or partnering with them and taking on the bulk of the development work. For example, if you must ingest data from a Postgres or MySQL database, get permission from the source team to implement streaming CDC with Debezium (see Chapter 4) rather than writing yet another ingestion job.

Reuse of Data Model Logic

Complexity can also arise further down a pipeline and in particular during data modeling in the transform phase of a pipeline (see Chapter 6). As analysts build more data models, they tend to do one of two things:

- Repeat logic in the SQL that builds each model.
- Derive models off of each other, creating numerous dependencies between models.

Just as code reuse is ideal in data ingestions (and software engineering in general), it's also ideal in data modeling. It ensures that a single source of truth exists and reduces the amount of code that needs to be changed in the case of a bug or business logic change. The trade-off is a more complex dependency graph in a pipeline.

Figure 9-1 shows a DAG (see Chapter 7) with a single data ingestion and four data models that are all built via scripts that run in parallel. They can be executed in that fashion because they have no dependencies on each other.

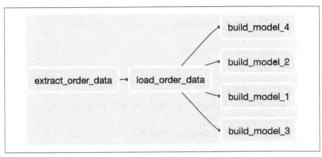

Figure 9-1. Four independent data models.

If they are truly unrelated data models, that is not a problem. However, if they all share some logic, then it's best to refactor the models and the DAG to look something like Figure 9-2.

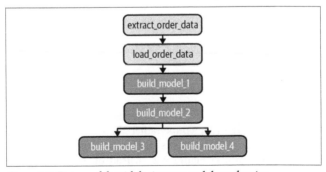

Figure 9-2. Data models with logic reuse and dependencies.

Example 9-2 shows a simple example of logic reuse that represents the script executed in the build_model_1 task in Figure 9-2. The script generates an order count by day and stores it in a data model called orders_by_day.

You can use the Orders table from Chapter 6, which can be re-created and populated with the following SQL:

```sql
CREATE TABLE Orders (
  OrderId int,
  OrderStatus varchar(30),
  OrderDate timestamp,
  CustomerId int,
  OrderTotal numeric
);

INSERT INTO Orders
  VALUES(1,'Shipped','2020-06-09',100,50.05);
INSERT INTO Orders
  VALUES(2,'Shipped','2020-07-11',101,57.45);
INSERT INTO Orders
  VALUES(3,'Shipped','2020-07-12',102,135.99);
INSERT INTO Orders
  VALUES(4,'Shipped','2020-07-12',100,43.00);
```

Example 9-2. model_1.sql

```sql
CREATE TABLE IF NOT EXISTS orders_by_day AS
SELECT
    CAST(OrderDate AS DATE) AS order_date,
    COUNT(*) AS order_count
FROM Orders
GROUP BY CAST(OrderDate AS DATE);
```

Subsequent models in the DAG can refer to this table when they need a daily order count rather than recalculating each time. Example 9-3 represents the script executed in the build_model_2 task in Figure 9-2. Instead of recalculating the order count by day, it uses the orders_by_day model instead. Though getting an order count by day may sound trivial, with more complex calculations or queries with additional logic in the WHERE clause or joins, it's even more important to write the logic once and reuse. Doing so ensures a single source of truth, ensures a single model to maintain, and, as a bonus, only requires your data warehouse to run any complex logic a single time and store the results for later reference. In some cases, that time savings is notable in a pipeline's runtime.

Example 9-3. model_2.sql

```
SELECT
  obd.order_date,
  ot.order_count
FROM orders_by_day obd
LEFT JOIN other_table ot
  ON ot.some_date = obd.order_date;
```

Though some savvy data analysts design their data models and the subsequent DAG in this way from the start, it's more common to find opportunity to refactor only after problems arise in a pipeline. For example, if a bug is found in the logic of a model and needs to be fixed in multiple models, then there is likely an opportunity to apply the logic to a single model and derive other models from it.

Though the end result is a more complex set of dependencies, if handled properly, as you'll see in the following section, you'll find the logic in the data modeling portion of your pipeline to be more reliable and less likely to result in multiple versions of truth.

Ensuring Dependency Integrity

As noted in the previous section, despite all of the benefits of reusing data model logic, there is a trade-off: the need to keep track of what models rely on each other and ensure that those dependencies are defined properly in a DAG for orchestration.

In Figure 9-2 in the previous section (and queries in Examples 9-2 and 9-3), model_2 is dependent on model_1, and model_3 and model_4 both depend on model_2. Those dependencies are defined properly in the DAG, but as teams build more models, keeping track of dependencies becomes quite a chore and prone to error.

As pipelines get more complex, it's time to consider programatic approaches to defining and validating dependencies between data models. There are a number of approaches, of which I'll discuss two.

First, you can build some logic into your development process to identify dependencies in SQL scripts and ensure that any tables that a script depends on are executed upstream in a DAG. Doing so isn't simple and can be done either by parsing out table names from a SQL script or, more commonly, requiring the data analyst writing the model to provide a list of dependencies manually in a config file when they submit a new model or modification to an existing one. In both cases, you have some work ahead of you and are adding some friction to your development process.

Another approach is to use a data model development framework like dbt (*https://www.getdbt.com*), which among other benefits has a mechanism for analysts to define references between models right in the SQL they write for the model definition.

More About dbt

dbt is an open source product created by Fishtown Analytics that has grown into a widely used and contributed-to tool in the data analytics community. It's written in Python and is easy to deploy and use on your own. There is also a commercial, fully hosted version called dbt Cloud if you'd rather not run it on your own. You can learn more about dbt by reading the official documentation (*https://oreil.ly/mTRPs*).

For example, I'll rewrite model_2.sql from Example 9-3 and use the ref() function in dbt to refer to model_1.sql in the join. Example 9-4 shows the result.

Example 9-4. model_2_dbt.sql

```
SELECT
  obd.order_date,
  ot.order_count
FROM {{ref('model_1')}} obd
LEFT JOIN other_table ot
  ON ot.some_date = obd.order_date;
```

Data Models in dbt

Data models in dbt are all defined as SELECT statements. Though similar to how data models were introduced in Chapter 6, dbt models can take advantage of functions like ref() via Jinja templating, which will be familiar to many Python developers.

With the updated SQL, dbt knows that model_2 relies on model_1 and ensures execution in the proper order. In fact, dbt builds a DAG dynamically rather than forcing you to do so in a tool like Airflow. When the data model is compiled by dbt prior to executing, the reference to model_1 is filled in with the table name (orders_by_day). If all four models from the DAG in Figure 9-2 are instead written in dbt, they can be compiled and executed with a single command on the command line:

```
$ dbt run
```

When dbt run is executed, the SQL scripts representing each model will run in the proper order based on how each table is referenced from each other. As you learned in Chapter 7, running command-line tasks in Airflow is simple. If you'd still like to use Airflow as your orchestrator alongside dbt for your data model development, that's no problem. Figure 9-3 shows an updated DAG where the two steps in the ingestion are run just like before. When they are completed, a single Airflow task executes the dbt run command, which handles executing the SQL for all four data models in the correct order.

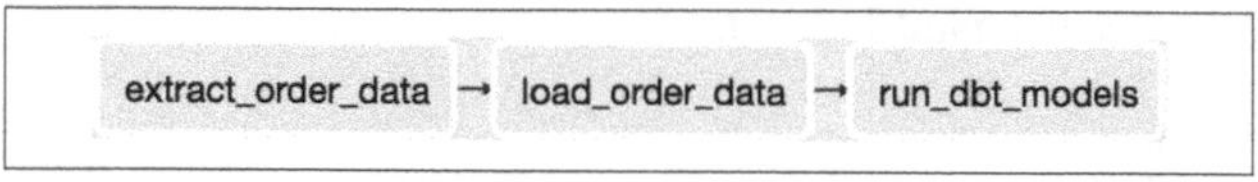

extract_order_data → load_order_data → run_dbt_models

Figure 9-3. Data models executed in dbt from Airflow.

Though in this example I'm running all models in the dbt project, you can specify a subset of models to run by passing parameters to dbt run as well.

Whether you choose to identify and validate model dependencies with custom code you inject into your development process, or leverage a product like dbt, handling dependencies at scale is key to maintaining a data pipeline. It's best not to leave it to manual checks and human eyes!

## CHAPTER 10

Measuring and Monitoring Pipeline Performance

Even the most well-designed data pipelines are not meant to be "set and forget." The practice of measuring and monitoring the performance of pipelines is essential. You owe it to your team and stakeholders to set, and live up to, expectations when it comes to the reliability of your pipelines.

This chapter outlines some tips and best practices for doing something that data teams deliver to others but surprisingly don't always invest in themselves: collecting data and measuring performance of their work.

Key Pipeline Metrics

Before you can determine what data you need to capture throughout your pipelines, you must first decide what metrics you want to track.

Choosing metrics should start with identifying what matters to you and your stakeholders. Some examples include the following:

- How many validation tests (see Chapter 8) are run, and what percent of the total tests run pass

- How frequently a specific DAG runs successfully

- The total runtime of a pipeline over the course of weeks, months, and years

---

How Many Metrics to Track?

Beware of a common trap: looking at too many metrics! Just as there is danger in relying on a single metric to tell the entire story of pipeline performance and reliability, too many metrics make it difficult to focus on what's most important. I suggest choosing two to three metrics at most to focus on. It's also important to ensure that they each have a unique purpose rather than overlapping in what they measure.

The good news is that gathering the data needed to calculate such metrics is within reach. As you'll see in the following sections, it's possible to capture this data directly from infrastructure built earlier in this book; in particular, see Airflow (Chapter 7) and the data validation framework (Chapter 8).

Prepping the Data Warehouse

Before you can monitor and report on the performance of your pipelines, you must of course capture the data required for such measurement. Thankfully, as a data professional you have the tools to do so right in front of you! Your data warehouse is the best place to store log data from each step in your data pipeline.

In this section, I define the structure of the tables you'll use to store data from Airflow and the data validation framework defined in Chapter 8. This data will later be used to develop the metrics essential to measuring pipeline performance.

I'd like to point out that there are numerous other data points you may want to track and report on. I like these two examples because they cover the basics and should inspire other tracking and measurements specific to your data infrastructure.

A Data Infrastructure Schema

First, you'll need a table to store the history of DAG runs from Airflow. Recall from Chapter 7 that Airflow is used to execute each step in a data pipeline. It also keeps the history of each DAG run. Before you extract that data, you need a table to load it into. The following is a definition for a table named dag_run_history. It should be created in your data warehouse in whatever schema you load data into during data ingestion:

```
CREATE TABLE dag_run_history (
    id int,
    dag_id varchar(250),
    execution_date timestamp with time zone,
    state varchar(250),
    run_id varchar(250),
    external_trigger boolean,
    end_date timestamp with time zone,
    start_date timestamp with time zone
);
```

In addition to reporting on the performance of DAGs, it's important to provide insight into data validity. In Chapter 8, I defined a simple, Python-based data validation framework. In this chapter I will extend it so that it logs the results of each validation test to the data warehouse. The following table, named validation_run_history, will be the destination of validation test results. I suggest creating it in the same schema of your data warehouse where ingested data lands upon load:

```
CREATE TABLE validation_run_history (
    script_1 varchar(255),
    script_2 varchar(255),
    comp_operator varchar(10),
    test_result varchar(20),
```

```
    test_run_at timestamp
);
```

The rest of this chapter implements the logic to populate and make use of the data loaded into the prior two tables.

Logging and Ingesting Performance Data

Now it's time to populate the two tables you created in your data warehouse in the previous section. The first will be populated by building a data ingestion job just like you learned about in Chapters 4 and 5. The second will require an enhancement to the data validation application first introduced in Chapter 8.

Ingesting DAG Run History from Airflow

To populate the dag_run_history table you created in your data warehouse in the previous section, you'll need to extract data from the Airflow application database you configured in "Apache Airflow Setup and Overview" on page 151.

In that section, I chose to use a Postgres database for Airflow to use, so the following extraction code follows the model defined in "Extracting Data from a PostgreSQL Database" on page 63. Note that I am choosing to load data incrementally, which is easy, thanks to the auto-incrementing id column of the dag_run table in the Airflow database. The output of this extraction (defined in Example 10-1) is a CSV file named *dag_run_extract.csv*, which is uploaded to the S3 bucket you set up in Chapter 4.

Before you execute the code, you'll need to add one new section to the *pipeline.conf* file from Chapter 4. As the following shows, it must contain the connection details for the Airflow database you set up in Chapter 7:

```
[airflowdb_config]
host = localhost
port = 5432
```

```
username = airflow
password = pass1
database = airflowdb
```

The Airflow REST API

Though I'm ingesting DAG run history directly from the Airflow application database, ideally I'd do so via an API or other layer of abstraction. In Airflow version 1.x, there is an "experimental" REST API that is quite limited and does not include an endpoint that supports the level of detail required for pipeline performance reporting. However, with Airflow 2.0 on the horizon, there is promise of an expanded and stable REST API. I suggest keeping an eye on the evolution of the Airflow API and consider ingesting from it, rather than the application database, in the future.

Example 10-1. airflow_extract.py

```python
import csv
import boto3
import configparser
import psycopg2

# get db Redshift connection info
parser = configparser.ConfigParser()
parser.read("pipeline.conf")
dbname = parser.get("aws_creds", "database")
user = parser.get("aws_creds", "username")
password = parser.get("aws_creds", "password")
host = parser.get("aws_creds", "host")
port = parser.get("aws_creds", "port")

# connect to the redshift cluster
rs_conn = psycopg2.connect(
            "dbname=" + dbname
            + " user=" + user
            + " password=" + password
```

```
              + " host=" + host
              + " port=" + port)

rs_sql = """SELECT COALESCE(MAX(id),-1)
              FROM dag_run_history;"""

rs_cursor = rs_conn.cursor()
rs_cursor.execute(rs_sql)
result = rs_cursor.fetchone()

# there's only one row and column returned
last_id = result[0]
rs_cursor.close()
rs_conn.commit()

# connect to the airflow db
parser = configparser.ConfigParser()
parser.read("pipeline.conf")
dbname = parser.get("airflowdb_config", "database")
user = parser.get("airflowdb_config", "username")
password = parser.get("airflowdb_config", "password")
host = parser.get("airflowdb_config", "host")
port =  parser.get("airflowdb_config", "port")
conn = psycopg2.connect(
        "dbname=" + dbname
        + " user=" + user
        + " password=" + password
        + " host=" + host
        + " port=" + port)

# get any new DAG runs. ignore running DAGs
m_query = """SELECT
                  id,
                  dag_id,
                  execution_date,
                  state,
                  run_id,
                  external_trigger,
                  end_date,
                  start_date
```

```
                FROM dag_run
                WHERE id > %s
                AND state <> \'running\';
                """

m_cursor = conn.cursor()
m_cursor.execute(m_query, (last_id,))
results = m_cursor.fetchall()

local_filename = "dag_run_extract.csv"
with open(local_filename, 'w') as fp:
    csv_w = csv.writer(fp, delimiter='|')
    csv_w.writerows(results)

fp.close()
m_cursor.close()
conn.close()

# load the aws_boto_credentials values
parser = configparser.ConfigParser()
parser.read("pipeline.conf")
access_key = parser.get("aws_boto_credentials",
                "access_key")
secret_key = parser.get("aws_boto_credentials",
                "secret_key")
bucket_name = parser.get("aws_boto_credentials",
                "bucket_name")

# upload the local CSV to the S3 bucket
s3 = boto3.client(
        's3',
        aws_access_key_id=access_key,
        aws_secret_access_key=secret_key)
s3_file = local_filename
s3.upload_file(local_filename, bucket_name, s3_file)
```

Once the extraction is complete, you can load the contents of the CSV file into your data warehouse as described in detail in Chapter 5. Example 10-2 defines how to do so if you have a Redshift data warehouse.

Example 10-2. airflow_load.py

```python
import boto3
import configparser
import pyscopg2

# get db Redshift connection info
parser = configparser.ConfigParser()
parser.read("pipeline.conf")
dbname = parser.get("aws_creds", "database")
user = parser.get("aws_creds", "username")
password = parser.get("aws_creds", "password")
host = parser.get("aws_creds", "host")
port = parser.get("aws_creds", "port")

# connect to the redshift cluster
rs_conn = psycopg2.connect(
            "dbname=" + dbname
            + " user=" + user
            + " password=" + password
            + " host=" + host
            + " port=" + port)

# load the account_id and iam_role from the conf files
parser = configparser.ConfigParser()
parser.read("pipeline.conf")
account_id = parser.get(
                "aws_boto_credentials",
                "account_id")
iam_role = parser.get("aws_creds", "iam_role")

# run the COPY command to ingest into Redshift
file_path = "s3://bucket-name/dag_run_extract.csv"

sql = """COPY dag_run_history
        (id,dag_id,execution_date,
        state,run_id,external_trigger,
        end_date,start_date)"""
sql = sql + " from %s "
sql = sql + " iam_role 'arn:aws:iam::%s:role/%s';"
```

```
# create a cursor object and execute the COPY command
cur = rs_conn.cursor()
cur.execute(sql,(file_path, account_id, iam_role))

# close the cursor and commit the transaction
cur.close()
rs_conn.commit()

# close the connection
rs_conn.close()
```

You may want to run the ingestion once manually, but you can later schedule it via an Airflow DAG as I describe in a later section of this chapter.

Adding Logging to the Data Validator

To log the results of the validation tests first introduced in Chapter 8, I'll add a function to the *validator.py* script called log_result. Because the script already connects to the data warehouse to run validation tests, I reuse the connection and simply INSERT a record with the test result:

```
def log_result(
    db_conn,
    script_1,
    script_2,
    comp_operator,
    result):

    m_query = """INSERT INTO
                 validation_run_history(
                   script_1,
                   script_2,
                   comp_operator,
                   test_result,
                   test_run_at)
                 VALUES(%s, %s, %s, %s,
                   current_timestamp);"""
```

```
    m_cursor = db_conn.cursor()
    m_cursor.execute(
      m_query,
      (script_1, script_2, comp_operator, result))
    db_conn.commit()

    m_cursor.close()
    db_conn.close()

    return
```

As a final modification, you'll need to call the new function after a test is run. Example 10-3 defines the updated validator in its entirety after the logging code is added. With this addition, each time a validation test is run, the result is logged in the validation_run_history table.

I suggest running a few validation tests to generate test data for examples that follow. For more on running validation tests, please refer to Chapter 8.

Example 10-3. validator_logging.py

```
import sys
import psycopg2
import configparser

def connect_to_warehouse():
    # get db connection parameters from the conf file
    parser = configparser.ConfigParser()
    parser.read("pipeline.conf")
    dbname = parser.get("aws_creds", "database")
    user = parser.get("aws_creds", "username")
    password = parser.get("aws_creds", "password")
    host = parser.get("aws_creds", "host")
    port = parser.get("aws_creds", "port")

    # connect to the Redshift cluster
    rs_conn = psycopg2.connect(
                "dbname=" + dbname
```

```
                        + " user=" + user
                        + " password=" + password
                        + " host=" + host
                        + " port=" + port)

        return rs_conn

# execute a test made of up two scripts
# and a comparison operator
# Returns true/false for test pass/fail
def execute_test(
        db_conn,
        script_1,
        script_2,
        comp_operator):

    # execute the 1st script and store the result
    cursor = db_conn.cursor()
    sql_file = open(script_1, 'r')
    cursor.execute(sql_file.read())

    record = cursor.fetchone()
    result_1 = record[0]
    db_conn.commit()
    cursor.close()

    # execute the 2nd script and store the result
    cursor = db_conn.cursor()
    sql_file = open(script_2, 'r')
    cursor.execute(sql_file.read())

    record = cursor.fetchone()
    result_2 = record[0]
    db_conn.commit()
    cursor.close()

    print("result 1 = " + str(result_1))
    print("result 2 = " + str(result_2))

    # compare values based on the comp_operator
```

```python
    if comp_operator == "equals":
        return result_1 == result_2
    elif comp_operator == "greater_equals":
        return result_1 >= result_2
    elif comp_operator == "greater":
        return result_1 > result_2
    elif comp_operator == "less_equals":
        return result_1 <= result_2
    elif comp_operator == "less":
        return result_1 < result_2
    elif comp_operator == "not_equal":
        return result_1 != result_2

    # if we made it here, something went wrong
    return False

def log_result(
        db_conn,
        script_1,
        script_2,
        comp_operator,
        result):
    m_query = """INSERT INTO
                    validation_run_history(
                        script_1,
                        script_2,
                        comp_operator,
                        test_result,
                        test_run_at)
                    VALUES(%s, %s, %s, %s,
                        current_timestamp);"""

    m_cursor = db_conn.cursor()
    m_cursor.execute(
                m_query,
                (script_1,
                    script_2,
                    comp_operator,
                    result)
            )
```

```python
        db_conn.commit()

        m_cursor.close()
        db_conn.close()

        return

if __name__ == "__main__":
    if len(sys.argv) == 2 and sys.argv[1] == "-h":
        print("Usage: python validator.py"
            + "script1.sql script2.sql "
            + "comparison_operator")
        print("Valid comparison_operator values:")
        print("equals")
        print("greater_equals")
        print("greater")
        print("less_equals")
        print("less")
        print("not_equal")

        exit(0)

    if len(sys.argv) != 5:
        print("Usage: python validator.py"
            + "script1.sql script2.sql "
            + "comparison_operator")
        exit(-1)

    script_1 = sys.argv[1]
    script_2 = sys.argv[2]
    comp_operator = sys.argv[3]
    sev_level = sys.argv[4]

    # connect to the data warehouse
    db_conn = connect_to_warehouse()

    # execute the validation test
    test_result = execute_test(
                    db_conn,
                    script_1,
```

```
                    script_2,
                    comp_operator)

# log the test in the data warehouse
log_result(
    db_conn,
    script_1,
    script_2,
    comp_operator,
    test_result)

print("Result of test: " + str(test_result))

if test_result == True:
    exit(0)
else:
    if sev_level == "halt":
        exit(-1)
    else:
        exit(0)
```

Logging at Scale

Though your data warehouse is an excellent place to store and
analyze performance data from your pipeline infrastructure, it's
not always best to send such data directly to it. If you intend to
produce a high volume of log data, such as the result of validation tests described in this section, it's worth considering first
routing it to log analysis infrastructure such as Splunk, Sumo-
Logic, or the open source ELK Stack (*https://oreil.ly/5ZYlY*)
(Elasticsearch, Logstash, and Kibana). Those platforms are
designed to perform well on a high volume of small write operations (as log entries tend to be), while data warehouses like
Snowflake and Redshift perform better ingesting data in bulk.
Once log data is sent to such a platform, you can later ingest it
in bulk into your data warehouse.

Most logging platforms have some form of analysis and visualization tooling included. I find such tooling preferable for analyzing log data in isolation and for operational monitoring and

reporting of the systems producing the logs. However, I still find it valuable to ingest log data into my data warehouse for further analysis, joining with nonlog sources, and displaying higher-level performance metrics in enterprise dashboards where non-engineers spend time. Thankfully, your organization may already have the necessary log analysis infrastructure up and running. In general, log analysis platforms complement data analytics infrastructure and are worth becoming familiar with.

For more on running validation tests, please see Chapter 8.

Transforming Performance Data

Now that you're capturing key events from your pipelines and storing them in your data warehouse, you can make use of them to report on pipeline performance. The best way to do that is to build a simple data pipeline!

Refer to the ELT pattern introduced in Chapter 3 and used throughout this book. The work to build a pipeline for reporting on the performance of each pipeline is nearly complete. The extract and load (EL) steps were taken care of in the previous section. All you have left is the transform (T) step. For this pipeline, that means turning the data from Airflow DAG runs, and other actions you've chosen to log, into the performance metrics you set out to measure and hold yourself accountable to.

In the following subsections, I define transformations to create data models for some of the key metrics discussed earlier in the chapter.

DAG Success Rate

As you'll recall from Chapter 6, you must consider the granularity of the data you want to model. In this case, I'd like to measure the success rate of each DAG by day. This level of granularity allows me to measure the success of either individual DAGs or multiple DAGs daily, weekly, monthly, or yearly. Whether the DAGs run once a day or more, this model will support a success rate. Example 10-4 defines the SQL to build the model. Note that this is a fully refreshed model for simplicity.

Example 10-4. dag_history_daily.sql

```
CREATE TABLE IF NOT EXISTS dag_history_daily (
  execution_date DATE,
  dag_id VARCHAR(250),
  dag_state VARCHAR(250),
  runtime_seconds DECIMAL(12,4),
  dag_run_count int
);

TRUNCATE TABLE dag_history_daily;

INSERT INTO dag_history_daily
  (execution_date, dag_id, dag_state,
  runtime_seconds, dag_run_count)
SELECT
  CAST(execution_date as DATE),
  dag_id,
  state,
  SUM(EXTRACT(EPOCH FROM (end_date - start_date))),
  COUNT(*) AS dag_run_count
FROM dag_run_history
GROUP BY
  CAST(execution_date as DATE),
  dag_id,
  state;
```

From the dag_history_daily table, you can measure the success rate of a single, or all DAGs, over a given date range. Here are a few examples based on runs of some DAGs defined in Chapter 7, but you'll see data based on your own Airflow DAG run history. Make sure to run at least one ingestion of Airflow

data (defined earlier in this chapter) to populate `dag_his
tory_daily`.

Here is a query to return the success rate by DAG. You can of
course filter to a given DAG or date range. Note that you must
CAST the `dag_run_count` as a `DECIMAL` to calculate a fractional
success rate:

```
SELECT
  dag_id,
  SUM(CASE WHEN dag_state = 'success' THEN 1
      ELSE 0 END)
      / CAST(SUM(dag_run_count) AS DECIMAL(6,2))
  AS success_rate
FROM dag_history_daily
GROUP BY dag_id;
```

The output of the query will look something like this:

```
dag_id             |        success_rate
-------------------+------------------------
tutorial           | 0.83333333333333333333
elt_pipeline_sample| 0.25000000000000000000
simple_dag         | 0.31250000000000000000
(3 rows)
```

DAG Runtime Change Over Time

Measuring the runtime of DAGs over time is often used to keep
track of DAGs that are taking longer to complete over time,
thus creating risk of data in the warehouse becoming stale. I'll
use the `dag_history_daily` table I created in the last subsection
to calculate the average runtime of each DAG by day.

Note that in the following query I only include successful DAG
runs, but you may want to report on long-running DAG runs
that failed (perhaps due to a timeout!) in some cases. Also keep
in mind that because multiple runs of a given DAG may occur
in a single day, I must average the runtimes of such DAGs in
the query.

Finally, because the `dag_history_daily` table is granular by date and `dag_state`, I don't really need to sum the `runtime_seconds` and `dag_run_count`, but as a best practice I do. Why? If I, or another analyst, decided to change the logic to do something like include failed DAG runs as well, then the `SUM()` function would be required, yet easily missed.

Here is the query for the `elt_pipeline_sample` DAG from Chapter 7:

```
SELECT
  dag_id,
  execution_date,
  SUM(runtime_seconds)
    / SUM(CAST(dag_run_count as DECIMAL(6,2)))
  AS avg_runtime
FROM dag_history_daily
WHERE
  dag_id = 'elt_pipeline_sample'
GROUP BY
  dag_id,
  execution_date
ORDER BY
dag_id,
execution_date;
```

The output of the query will look something like this:

```
dag_id              | execution_date |   avg_runtime
--------------------+----------------+----------
elt_pipeline_sample | 2020-09-16     |   63.773900
elt_pipeline_sample | 2020-09-17     |  105.902900
elt_pipeline_sample | 2020-09-18     |  135.392000
elt_pipeline_sample | 2020-09-19     |  101.111700
(4 rows)
```

Validation Test Volume and Success Rate

Thanks to the additional logging you added to the data validator earlier in this chapter, it's now possible to measure the success rate of validation tests, as well as the overall volume of tests run.

Test Volume in Context

Both success rate and test volume are worth monitoring, though I suggest also putting the test volume into context. The specifics of that are a bit out of scope for this chapter, but in general, the number of validation tests run should be proportional to the number of DAG tasks run. In other words, you should ensure that you're testing each step in your pipelines. What's a proper ratio of tests to pipeline step (often measured by DAG task)? That depends on how complex your steps are. Simple ingestion steps might require a single test to check for duplicate rows, while some transform steps are worthy of several tests to check for various context-specific errors.

Example 10-5 defines a new data model called `validator_sum mary_daily` that calculates and stores the results of each validator test at daily granularity.

Example 10-5. validator_summary_daily.sql

```
CREATE TABLE IF NOT EXISTS validator_summary_daily (
  test_date DATE,
  script_1 varchar(255),
  script_2 varchar(255),
  comp_operator varchar(10),
  test_composite_name varchar(650),
  test_result varchar(20),
  test_count int
);

TRUNCATE TABLE validator_summary_daily;

INSERT INTO validator_summary_daily
  (test_date, script_1, script_2, comp_operator,
  test_composite_name, test_result, test_count)
```

```
SELECT
  CAST(test_run_at AS DATE) AS test_date,
  script_1,
  script_2,
  comp_operator,
  (script_1
    || ' '
    || script_2
    || ' '
    || comp_operator) AS test_composite_name,
  test_result,
  COUNT(*) AS test_count
FROM validation_run_history
GROUP BY
  CAST(test_run_at AS DATE),
  script_1,
  script_2,
  comp_operator,
  (script_1 || ' ' || script_2 || ' ' || comp_opera
tor),
  test_result;
```

Though the logic to create `validator_summary_daily` is fairly
straightforward, it's worth calling out the `test_composite_name`
column. In the absence of a unique name for each validation
test (an enhancement worth considering), `test_compo
site_name` is the combination of the two scripts and operator
for the test. It acts as a composite key that can be used to group
validation test runs. For example, here is the SQL to calculate
the percentage of time that each test passes. You can of course
look at this by day, week, month, or any other time range you'd
like:

```
SELECT
  test_composite_name,
  SUM(
    CASE WHEN test_result = 'true' THEN 1
    ELSE 0 END)
    / CAST(SUM(test_count) AS DECIMAL(6,2))
  AS success_rate
```

```
FROM validator_summary_daily
GROUP BY
  test_composite_name;
```

The output will look something like this:

```
test_composite_name        |       success_rate
---------------------------+----------------------
sql1.sql sql2.sql equals   | 0.33333333333333333
sql3.sql sql4.sql not_equal | 0.75000000000000000

(2 rows)
```

As for the volume of test runs, you may want to view this by date, test, or both. As noted earlier, it's important to keep this value in context. As you grow the number and complexity of your pipelines, you can use this measure to ensure that you're keeping up on testing the validity of data throughout pipelines. The following SQL produces both the test count and the success rate by date. This is a dataset that you can plot on a double y-axis line chart or similar visualization:

```
SELECT
  test_date,
  SUM(
    CASE WHEN test_result = 'true' THEN 1
    ELSE 0 END)
    / CAST(SUM(test_count) AS DECIMAL(6,2))
  AS success_rate,
  SUM(test_count) AS total_tests
FROM validator_summary_daily
GROUP BY
  test_date
ORDER BY
  test_date;
```

The results will look something like this:

```
test_date  |       success_rate        | total_tests
-----------+---------------------------+-----------
2020-11-03 | 0.33333333333333333333333 |     3
2020-11-04 | 1.00000000000000000000000 |     6
```

(3 row)

Orchestrating a Performance Pipeline

With the code from the previous sections in hand, you can create a new Airflow DAG to schedule and orchestrate a pipeline to ingest and transform the pipeline performance data. It may feel a bit recursive, but you can use the existing infrastructure you have for this type of operation. Keep in mind that this backward-looking reporting focused on insights and not something mission critical like uptime monitoring or alerting on pipelines. You never want to use the same infrastructure to do that!

The Performance DAG

A DAG to orchestrate all of the steps defined in this chapter will look familiar based on examples from Chapter 7. Per Example 10-3, the results from the validation tests are already logging in the data warehouse. That means that there are only a few steps needed in this pipeline:

1. Extract data from the Airflow database (per Example 10-1).
2. Load data from the Airflow extract into the warehouse (per Example 10-2).
3. Transform the Airflow history (per Example 10-4).
4. Transform the data validation history (per Example 10-5).

Example 10-6 is the source for the Airflow DAG, and Figure 10-1 shows the DAG in graph form.

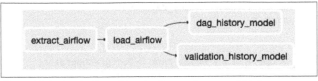

Figure 10-1. Graph view of the pipeline_performance DAG.

Example 10-6. pipeline_performance.py

```python
from datetime import timedelta
from airflow import DAG
from airflow.operators.bash_operator \
    import BashOperator
from airflow.operators.postgres_operator \
    import PostgresOperator
from airflow.utils.dates import days_ago

dag = DAG(
    'pipeline_performance',
    description='Performance measurement pipeline',
    schedule_interval=timedelta(days=1),
    start_date = days_ago(1),
)

extract_airflow_task = BashOperator(
    task_id='extract_airflow',
    bash_command='python /p/airflow_extract.py',
    dag=dag,
)

load_airlflow_task = BashOperator(
    task_id='load_airflow',
    bash_command='python /p/airflow_load.py',
    dag=dag,
)

dag_history_model_task = PostgresOperator(
    task_id='dag_history_model',
    postgres_conn_id='redshift_dw',
```

```
        sql='/sql/dag_history_daily.sql',
        dag=dag,
)

validation_history_model_task = PostgresOperator(
    task_id='validation_history_model',
    postgres_conn_id='redshift_dw',
    sql='/sql/validator_summary_daily.sql',
    dag=dag,
)

extract_airflow_task >> load_airlflow_task
load_airlflow_task >> dag_history_model_task
load_airlflow_task >> validation_history_model_task
```

Performance Transparency

With a working pipeline to measure the performance of your production pipelines and data validation tests, there's one last thing to keep in mind: sharing the resulting insights with your data team and stakeholders. Transparency of the pipeline performance is key to building trust with stakeholders and creating a sense of ownership and pride on your team.

Here are a few tips for making use of the data and insights generated throughout this chapter:

Leverage visualization tools
> Make the metrics from the data models you created accessible in the same visualization tools that your stakeholders use. That might be Tableau, Looker, or a similar product. Whatever it is, make sure it's where stakeholders and your team are going every day, anyway.

Share summarized metrics regularly
> Share summarized metrics at least monthly (if not weekly) via email, Slack, or some other place that your team and stakeholders keep an eye on.

Watch trends, not just current values

Both on dashboards and summaries you share, don't just share the latest values of each metric. Include change over time as well, and ensure that negative trends are pointed out as often as positive ones.

React to trends

Sharing trends in metrics isn't just for show. It's an opportunity to react and improve. Are validation tests failing at a higher rate than the month before? Dig into why, make changes, and watch future trends to measure the impact of your work.

Index

About the Author

James Densmore is the director of data infrastructure at HubSpot as well as the founder and principal consultant at Data Liftoff. He has more than 10 years of experience leading data teams and building data infrastructure at Wayfair, O'Reilly Media, HubSpot, and Degreed. James has a BS in computer science from Northeastern University and an MBA from Boston College.

Colophon

The bird on the cover of *Data Pipelines Pocket Reference* is a white-browed babbler (*Pomatostomus superciliosus*). The word *superciliosus* comes from the Latin *supercilium*, or *eyebrow*, a reference to the bird's most distinguishing feature.

White-browed babblers have white browlines and throats. Their plumage ranges from gray-brown to dark brown. They are the smallest of Australia's babblers at 6 to 8 inches in length, with long tails and short wings. These babblers spend most of their time foraging in southern Australia's woodlands for insects, crustaceans, fruit, seeds, and nuts.

Unlike most birds, white-browed babblers build two nests: one for roosting and one for incubating their eggs. The birds are very social, making so much noise in large groups that Australians also call them the chatterer, cackler, or yahoo.

White-browed babblers have a status of Least Concern from the IUCN. Many of the animals on O'Reilly's covers are endangered; all of them are important to the world.

The cover illustration is by Karen Montgomery, based on a black and white *Encyclopedie D'Histoire Naturelle* engraving. The cover fonts are Gilroy Semibold and Guardian Sans. The text font is Adobe Minion Pro, headings are Adobe Myriad Condensed, and code is Dalton Maag's Ubuntu Mono.